Overcoming Spiritual Depression

Overcoming Spiritual Depression

by Arie Elshout

Translated by
Bartel Elshout

REFORMATION HERITAGE BOOKS
Grand Rapids, Michigan

Original Title: *Nogmaals een Helpende Hand*

Copyright © 2006

REFORMATION HERITAGE BOOKS
2965 Leonard St., NE
Grand Rapids, MI 49525
616-977-0599 / Fax 616-285-3246
e-mail: orders@heritagebooks.org
website: www.heritagebooks.org

10 digit ISBN #1-892777-93-2
13 digit ISBN #978-1-892777-93-5

For additional Reformed literature, both new and used, request a free book list from Reformation Heritage Books at the above address.

Table of Contents

Preface

With grateful memory, I write this prefatory word at the request of the translator, Rev. Bartel Elshout, son of the author, Rev. Arie Elshout (1923-1991), who was used greatly by God in my teen years as pastor in Kalamazoo, Michigan, to lead a goodly number of my peers and myself to spiritual liberty in Christ Jesus. What a God-sent help he was to many of us young pilgrims, directing us to the glorious Savior and teaching us the way to the celestial city! Yet, even as he endeared himself to us through his faithful and courageous Christ-exalting ministry, he himself was led by God through deep ways of spiritual warfare and depression during his Kalamazoo pastorate. God subsequently sanctified these trials in his life so that he would be used to console hundreds of people, both in personal counsel and through his books, with the comfort that he himself was comforted of God (2 Cor. 1:4). This book, now ably translated into English, is an important contribution to his compassionate and comforting ministry. Its companion volume, *A Helping Hand* (Grand Rapids: Reformation Heritage Books, 1997), has already assisted scores of people.

Overcoming Spiritual Depression is packed with godly wisdom and heartfelt compassion for Christians who are battling the Elijah syndrome of discouragement. It is also a healing tonic for those who have loved ones suffering from this spiritual, emotional, and psychological malady. The dos and don'ts of how to respond to the suffering are expounded, in a most engaging way, from Elijah and the author's experience under the juniper tree (1 Kings 19). Concise yet thorough, practical yet spiritual, this book opens up the world of depression such that both the depressed and those closely associated with them will be gripped and liberated by the author's many enlightening insights. Every minister, office-bearer, and caring believer should read it to learn how to counsel and interact with those who are spiritually cast down and emotionally depleted.

May God graciously use this English translation as powerfully as He used the frequently reprinted Dutch volume for the disburdening and "lifting up of the downcast," fulfilling Psalm 43:5, "Why art thou cast down, O my soul? and why art thou disquieted within me? hope in God: for I shall yet praise him, who is the health of my countenance, and my God."

— Joel R. Beeke

Translator's Note

Since the publication of the translation of my father's first book, *A Helping Hand*, there have been frequent requests that the sequel to this book, *Nogmaals een Helpende Hand* (*Once more a Helping Hand*), be translated as well. Having promised my father just prior to his death that I would translate all the books he has written, I hereby wish to fulfill this obligation. It is my earnest prayer that this book may also prove to be a blessing to many, and that office-bearers may especially glean much instruction from it. May the God who led my father through a deep valley of affliction, but also delivered him from this horrible pit, use this book to comfort others with the comfort with which He comforted my father.

— Bartel Elshout

Author's Preface

The publication of this book is motivated by my compassion for those who wrestle with problems of a psychological nature. The many grateful reactions to my previous book, *A Helping Hand*, prompted me to extend a helping hand once more to those burdened by these problems.

It is important that those who suffer, as well as those who are called to counsel them, have a correct understanding of the causes of mental suffering. The reading of a book such as this could be helpful in preventing depressions that are symptomatic of a different problem in someone's life. An ounce of prevention is worth more than a pound of cure.

In 1 Kings 19, we find a description of a crisis in the life of the prophet Elijah. I believe that this portion of Scripture yields instruction regarding what causes certain types of depressions, as well as the means whereby a person can be delivered from them. This book will study how 1 Kings 19 records for us one man's experience in the valleys that all believers go through in the life of faith. Elijah emerged from this crisis as a purified and seasoned man, and others can as well. The God who delivered Elijah from his misery still lives!

It is the prayer and wish of the writer that the LORD would use this book to deliver people who are in need, so that all glory goes to Him who is wonderful in counsel and excellent in His works (Isa. 28:29).

—1—
From Strength to Complaint

The prophet Elijah is not only a man whose history is recorded in the Bible, but also a man who struggled with depression.

There are professionals who apply the term "depressive" only to people who are either mentally disturbed or who suffer from a serious psychological disorder. Other professionals use this term in a much wider sense. It is in the latter sense that I wish to designate Elijah's condition as depressive.

We may and must be thankful for the fact that, in His Word, the Lord does not only focus on Elijah on the mountain peak of the life of faith. God's Spirit has deemed it beneficial and necessary to also focus on him as a man of like passion as we are, wrestling with fear and problems that seem to defy solution. This hero of faith, who did great things in the might of God (see 1 Kings 17 and 18), is set before us in 1 Kings 19 as a man who suffers from battle fatigue and who is weary of life itself—a man who has but one wish: to fall asleep, never to awake again. Who would have thought that a powerful man such as Elijah, shortly after what had transpired on Mount Carmel, could be so depressed that he would pray, "It is enough;

now, O LORD, take away my life, for I am not better than my fathers" (1 Kings 19:4)?

Just as many could never imagine that they could be subject to such a serious depression, it is most probable that Elijah also did not count on this possibility. The wish expressed by Elijah was preceded by a period of great fear, anxiety, and restlessness. The one gave birth to the other, which is usually the case. Therefore, the record of 1 Kings 19 contains a wealth of instruction for people who suffer from depression, and for those who are called to counsel and guide people who are thus afflicted.

In 1 Kings 17 and 18, we meet Elijah as a man who is full of the strength of the Lord. These chapters show us how God's Spirit can transform a son of man into a man who is very zealous for the honor of the Lord and for His kingdom. 1 Kings 19, however, shows us a man of like passions as we are—a man who was fearful and frail, who suffered from battle fatigue, and who was spiritually paralyzed by fear.

Many have asked themselves how it is possible that Elijah could descend so quickly from a mountain peak to a valley so deep that words fail us to describe its depth. Many depressed persons and their relatives have asked themselves how it is possible that they or others could have come into such circumstances that the tensions and problems of religious, domestic, social, and ecclesiastical life can no longer be processed in a normal fashion.

Upon reviewing the biographical data of Elijah's life, one can conclude that he was not a man who did a half job. He abhorred half-hearted measures. For him it was either doing something well or not doing it at all. He was not a man who halted between two opinions.

It can be a good personality trait to be precise, conscientious, and detail-oriented in everything one does. A keen sense of duty and responsibility can also be a very good thing. However, combined with someone's personality structure and other circumstances, this can produce such psychological stress that it leads to being overstressed. When a person, motivated either by pride or a desire to suppress or overcome feelings of inferiority, always demands excellence of himself, it will sooner or later lead to being overstressed, which can lead to depression.

From Elijah's words, "Now, O LORD, take away my life, for I am not better than my fathers," we could conclude that it had been his desire and goal to be better than his fathers. It can be a personality trait to desire and strive to be better than others and to do everything better than others. Ambition is as much a sin as avarice. Ambition is a hard taskmaster which never says, "It is enough." This hard taskmaster has ruined the lives of many.

It is, however, also possible that the desire to be better in all things than others and to do all things better than others proceeds from religious training. We know that God's law demands of us perfect obedience to all God's commandments. The desire to live in harmony with God's Word and thus be void of offense can be a very good desire—that is, if it proceeds from the root of a childlike desire to fear the Lord. A faith that aims for God's honor and the well-being of our neighbor and works by love, as well as strives to always have a conscience void of offense before God and man, is the fruit of the work of the Holy Spirit.

In that sense, it is commendable when someone desires to be better than those who do not take God's honor and will very seriously. In fact, the more love there is in someone's heart toward a God who, for Christ's sake, is so good to wretched men, the more zeal there will be to strive to resist sin in one's self and others, and to promote righteousness in ourselves and others. We must continually examine ourselves before the countenance of God regarding the motive of our actions and what our objective is in pursuing perfection. Even in the greatest of the saints there are remnants of legalism which can lead to bondage or stress.

The Bible says that Elijah was a man of like passions as we are. I do not know whether Elijah's striving to be better than his fathers was contaminated by unholy ambition. I do know, however, that being overstressed and depressed can in some cases also be caused by the aforementioned factors. Watchfulness and prayer are of the essence here! In our striving to be perfect, our intentions can be so good, but that ambition which renders us unable or unwilling to accept the fact that we cannot achieve perfection is an evil from which we must be delivered.

Our apparent zeal is too often a cover-up for our natural aversion to being beggars at the throne of grace. It is not easy to conclude that we naturally despise being dependent upon grace. When we detect this within ourselves, it ought to lead us to humility rather than despair, for enemies are reconciled with God by the death and grace of the Lord Jesus Christ. He came to save sinners and He teaches us to pray by His Spirit, "O God, be merciful to me a sinner." Such prayers the Lord desires to hear and answer.

What Preceded Elijah's Depression

As we attempt to answer the question of how Elijah ended up in a condition of such despondency (1 Kings 19:4), we must first of all consider what preceded it.

This anxiety and despondency was preceded by a very stressful period. We may safely assume that Elijah had gradually prepared for his encounter with Ahab. The Spirit's work to equip Elijah in solitude for his public ministry obviously had an effect upon him. The words, "As the LORD God of Israel liveth, before whom I stand, there shall not be dew nor rain these years, but according to my word" (1 Kings 17:1), were uttered with explosive force.

When we are called upon to perform a demanding task, it takes its toll on our bodies—even if the Lord has called and equipped us in an extraordinary manner to do so. The great tension which this sometimes generates will be very taxing on our psyche. Since Elijah was a man of like passions as we are, his stress level must have been very high before and during his encounters with Ahab.

Performing a task that demands a high level of psychological energy—such as when great demands are made on us as a result of domestic, work-related, or church-related stress—can easily lead to being overstressed if not counterbalanced by rest and relaxation. A bow which is always drawn will ultimately break.

At times, finding time for relaxation can be impossible. However, it can also be true that we neglect opportunities to relax or even avoid them. Sometimes we take refuge in our work for fear of having to come to grips with ourselves. This can lead to being addicted to work, which is unquestionably detrimental to our psychological and physical well-being. The price of such foolishness is often very high. Constant work will sooner or later lead to being overstressed; being overstressed in turn leads to other problems such as being incapable of doing our work for a shorter or longer period of time.

The first and second encounters between Elijah and Ahab were separated by a period of three years and six months. By the goodness of the Lord, his stay at the brook Cherith and with the widow of Zarephath provided Elijah with the necessary relaxation after a period of great stress regarding his first encounter with Ahab.

The deep depression from which Elijah suffered and which led to his petition, "Now, O LORD, take away my life, for I am not better than my fathers," was precipitated by Elijah's second encounter with Ahab, as well as by what subsequently occurred on Mount Carmel.

The Sequence of Events on Mount Carmel

What transpired upon Mount Carmel may safely be labeled the climax of Elijah's life. In 1 Kings 18:36 we read, "Let it be known this day that thou art God in Israel, and that I am thy servant, and that I have done all these things at thy word." From this we know that everything Elijah did on Mount Carmel was done in harmony with what God had told him. We also know that God made it known that He was God in Israel and that Elijah was His servant. Who can express in words what it must have been like for Elijah when, in response to the answer God gave upon Elijah's prayer, the entire nation prostrated itself and cried out, "The Lord, he is the God; the Lord, he is the God!" (18:39). What amazement, adoration, and joy must have filled the heart of Elijah when he heard these words!

Elijah must have been exceedingly joyful when the people did more than just speak the words and, upon his invitation, took hold of Baal's priests whom they had never dared to touch. The journey from the brook Kishon and the slaughter of the four hundred fifty prophets of Baal was the culmination of what had transpired thus far. We cannot even begin to imagine what physical and psychological demands this must have made upon Elijah. I am sure that it must have been considerable. In addition, the time that Elijah spent on Mount Carmel after the slaughter of the prophets of Baal, supplicating for rain, must have been taxing for him. Processing all these things must have pushed him to his limits.

Considering what transpired that evening, we may safely conclude that Elijah's psychological reserves were nearly depleted after the dramatic events of this climactic day in his life.

Upon Every Climax Follows a Valley

It is well-known that highs in our lives are followed by lows. Every climax triggers a reaction—sometimes even an anti-climax. After a series of dramatic events in a short period of time, one will be especially vulnerable to a psychological slump. Periods of depression can often be explained by what preceeds them.

No one would blame a blown electrical fuse if the fuse failed due to excessive demands being made on it. Neither would we do so if the fuse failed because of a short in the line. This is perfectly normal. However, when someone's psychological fuses blow due to excessive stress or emotional short-circuiting, the reactions are often quite different. Frequently, people try to establish a cause-effect relationship between experiencing a breakdown and a given sin. This ought not to be. Which sin did Elijah commit that would explain his depression to be a punishment upon it? Did he think too highly of himself and of the importance of his work? That is indeed possible, for he was a man of like passions as we are. I do not believe, however, that we may make such a connection. Did he do something for which he could justly be rebuked? I believe not. And yet, after having had a spiritual mountain-peak experience, he descended into a very deep pit. He was neither the first nor the last person to have such an experience. Did the Lord tempt him above what he was able to bear? No; otherwise he would never have come out of this pit.

Through his mountain-peak experiences, Elijah learned how great, glorious, and faithful the Lord is. In the deep valleys he had to learn how small, insignificant, sinful, and helpless he was. He was a man of like passions as all others who had to learn to live by grace alone—and who, out of the fullness of Christ, received grace for grace. In order that he would not exalt himself because of what he had experienced on Mount Carmel, he came into the situation so well known to us. All that happened to Elijah was not meant for his destruction, but for his benefit and the benefit of others. It was love, not wrath, that moved God to direct things in this fashion, so that the Lord would be glorified and Elijah would prosper spiritually. That is evident from what followed Elijah's depression. Many throughout history have learned to see their suffering in that light. Its purpose is to yield knowledge of self and of God, make and keep one humble, and lead to glorifying God and His ways. The petition from Psalm 38, "Forsake me not, O LORD: O my God, be not far from me. Make haste to help me, O Lord my salvation" (vv. 21-22), is a petition the Lord wants to hear from the lips of those who suffer. When that prayer is answered, people can even thank the Lord for having experienced such depression.

Recently I saw a stone attached to a branch of an apple tree. The owner of the orchard had attached the stone to help the branch grow in such a fashion that it would yield the maximum amount of fruit. The stone was necessary to make the branch fulfill the purpose intended by the grower, and it prevented the branch from growing in a direction that would not be subservient to fruitfulness.

In seeing the stone attached to the branch, I observed a picture of how the Lord deals with many people. In His love and wisdom, the Lord frequently uses difficulties to prevent growth in the wrong direction. The fruits He wants to produce are those worthy of repentance—all to His honor, and to the salvation of ourselves and others.

By way of His Word, Spirit, and providence, God will see to it that people will fulfill His purpose. To that end, He has laid help upon One who is mighty, Jesus Christ, by whose hand the pleasure of the Lord will prosper—and to accomplish this, He will not spare our flesh and blood.

May the Lord teach us to view our trials in that light! That light is a wondrous light; it drives away all darkness and causes us to worship Him in holy adoration, for He is wonderful in counsel and excellent in working (Isa. 28:29). All of this is beautifully expressed in the following poem:

He Maketh No Mistake

My Father's way may twist and turn,
My heart may throb and ache,
But in my soul I'm glad I know,
He maketh no mistake.

My cherished plans may go astray,
My hope may fade away,
But still I'll trust my Lord to lead,
For He doth know the way.

Tho' night be dark and it may seem,
That day will never break;
I'll pin my faith, my all in Him.
He maketh no mistake.

There's so much now I cannot see,
My eyesight's far too dim;
But come what may, I'll simply trust
And leave it all to Him.

And by and by the mist will lift
And plain it all He'll make.
Through all the way, tho' dark to me,
He made not one mistake
— A. M. Overton

Many Straws Will Break the Camel's Back

A state of depression, whether or not of a clinical nature, can rarely be attributed to a single cause. There is usually a straw that will break the camel's back. However, there is usually a complex array of circumstances which had already put much stress on the camel's back. A depressed person will frequently focus only on what caused the camel's back to break without considering the other factors that contributed to the development of the crisis.

It belongs to the task of professionals to identify these factors and, to the benefit of the one who is in need of help, to find ways to address them. Sometimes these factors are only the result of psychological overload. Sometimes there are physical causes that have contributed to a depression that can even be of a clinical nature. Frequently one's circumstances can be attributed to both psychological and physical factors. When our circumstances are of such a nature that they result in mental and physical exhaustion, it is almost impossible to avoid problems.

In the preceding, I have attempted to demonstrate that what happened on Mount Carmel must have made extraordinary demands on Elijah's psyche. That alone would have been sufficient to trigger the condition in which Elijah found himself. Upon a careful reading of 1 Kings 18, it will become evident that also physical exhaustion played a role in fostering the situation of which we read in 1 Kings 19.

In 1 Kings 18:40, we read the simple and yet dramatic statement, "And Elijah brought them (i.e. the 450 prophets of Baal) down to the brook Kishon, and slew them there." This massacre probably took place in a relatively short period of time. If Elijah single-handedly killed the 450 prophets of Baal, as the text appears to indicate, then it will have drained him of much physical energy. During this massacre, he will probably not have noticed how this sapped his strength. He proceeded to kill these priests of Baal until not a single one of them was left. This task had to be completed at all costs. He probably did not give himself a moment's rest until all 450 priests of Baal had been killed.

If it was indeed true that Elijah single-handedly killed the 450 priests of Baal, the question could be asked why he did not delegate part of this task to others. I do not know whether Elijah was someone who only had confidence in what he did himself—who neither could, dared to, nor would delegate anything to someone else. This can be the result of one's personality and/or certain circumstances.

There are people who have such an inferiority complex that, in order to have any measure of self-respect, they will try to do everything themselves. They are of the opinion that delegation to others is a sign of weakness or incompetency—or could be interpreted as such. Instead of asking others to help them or to accept offered help, they make unreasonable and even impossible demands on themselves.

There are also people who are too proud to delegate work to others. They have such great confidence in their own knowledge and ability that they will not entrust anything to someone else.

Finally, there are also people who are too ambitious to let others participate in the work they are doing. Even though they lack the time to complete a given task in a calm manner, they will not delegate. Their ambition does not permit them to delegate anything to someone else. They would rather dig in a bit deeper to complete everything on time.

It testifies of wisdom when, in a timely fashion, we seek the help of others when for any given reason we are not able to complete the task at hand. It is not easy to do this, particularly not for people who have a great sense of responsibility. Failure to do so, however, will yield nothing but grief, In doing so, we shortchange ourselves. When we reject offers of help by those who perceive that we cannot handle a given task by ourselves, we are also shortchanging the other person.

It is contrary to the Lord's will that we shortchange either ourselves or others. Instead, we may—yes, must—ask for and accept help when our circumstances necessitate this.

When we add to the massacre that which is recorded in 1 Kings 18:46, we get even clearer insight into the contributing factors to what transpired on the evening of the day on which such glorious things were experienced by Elijah. In verse 46 we are told that, while a great rain came down upon the parched land, Elijah "girded up his loins, and ran before Ahab to the entrance of Jezreel." By paying homage to the king, Elijah evidently wished to demonstrate that he was not a revolutionary who refused to render appropriate honor to his sovereign. The hand of the LORD was upon Elijah; that is, the Spirit of the Lord filled Elijah's heart. When the latter is the case, it will be self-evident that one pays homage to those to whom such honor is due by virtue of their public or ecclesiastical position—albeit that we despise the sins of such persons. It is not a fruit of grace but rather of the flesh when one fails to render homage to those who have been placed over us.

It ought to be obvious that running in front of Ahab's chariot demanded a great deal of physical energy from Elijah who probably was not accustomed to such exercise. Elijah's mind and body had to be pushed to their limits to keep Elijah from collapsing before Ahab's chariot. (One can hardly imagine that the horses of Ahab's chariot walked at a slow pace.) Furthermore, the distance that he had to traverse was about 25 km (17 miles).

After all this had been accomplished, Elijah was exhausted. This can be deduced from what followed upon the reception of Jezebel's message that he would be killed the following day.

No one should think that no mental or physical energy is expended in the performance of a task in which one experiences the Lord's anointing and assistance and which is performed with delight. The opposite is evident in Elijah's life. Paul's words that we have this treasure in earthen vessels (2 Cor. 4:7) also articulate this clearly.

Would it be fair to rebuke Elijah for having exerted himself excessively on that day, implying that it was therefore his own fault that he became seriously depressed? Time and again it occurs that the question of guilt comes on the table when people suffer from burnout. This is wrong! It can very well be that burnout and depression are connected with exhaustion rather than guilt. Such was the case with Elijah. It was in the fulfillment of his obligation that he became mentally and physically exhausted. Let us not rebuke when rebukes are not called for. This applies to those who suffer from depression as well as those who are called upon to interact with depressed individuals.

Elijah's history also confirms that it is simply not true what some suggest, namely, that a healthy spiritual life precludes the possibility of becoming seriously depressed. Did not Elijah demonstrate on Mount Carmel that his spiritual life was healthy? Did he not live close to the Lord on the eve of the day when he panicked as a result of the message that came to him from Jezebel? Elijah's troubles were caused by physical rather than spiritual circumstances.

God's Word teaches that "there is one event to the righteous, and to the wicked" (Eccl. 9:2). Also in regard to these matters, "let him that thinketh he standeth take heed lest he fall" (1 Cor. 10:12). So many have been of the opinion that something of this nature could never happen to them. Reality taught them otherwise. Such an experience will cure us from judging others harshly.

—2—
How Are We to Judge Complaints?

We read in Psalm 41:1 that "blessed is he that considereth the poor." In light of the original Hebrew, we could paraphrase this as follows: Blessed is he who deals circumspectly or wisely with those who are in need.

Many are the miseries to which humanity is subjected due to sin. Though there are many who treat needy individuals as the priest and the Levite treated the proverbial Samaritan, yet, by the grace of God, there are some who do take the plight of needy individuals to heart and who are committed to do whatever they can to resolve the needs of those who suffer—or, if that is not possible, to alleviate their suffering.

Job, the great sufferer of the Old Testament, once uttered the heart-rending cry, "Have pity upon me, have pity upon me, O ye my friends; for the hand of God hath touched me" (Job 19:21). The friends of Job are to be commended for the fact that they visited him soon after he was overcome by grief and sorrow. However, not much came of their intent "to mourn with him and to comfort him" (Job 2:11). They undoubtedly came to Job with the best intentions, addressing him (also with the best intentions) as we find it recorded in Scripture. However, their words intensified Job's suffering rather than alleviating it.

When they heard Job curse the day of his birth, as well as the words he uttered regarding what had befallen him, they were not able to sympathize with him. The more Job spoke, the more perplexed his friends became. They could not understand how a man who previously had instructed many and had strengthened the weak hands, whose words upheld him that was falling and strengthened the feeble knees (Job 4:3-4), who in both word and deed had exemplified godliness in such a manner that he adorned the church of God, could conduct himself as he did in his affliction.

The words of Eliphaz, "But now it is come upon thee, and thou faintest; it toucheth thee, and thou art troubled" (Job 4:5), must have wounded Job's soul deeply. Did not Eliphaz speak the truth after all? Yes, he certainly did, but he could and should have addressed Job in a different manner—not so haughtily and mercilessly. In speaking to Job about God and His ways, these friends undoubtedly meant to do what was best for Job. Nevertheless the Lord's assessment was that they had not spoken rightly of Him, and in doing so they caused His wrath to be kindled against them (Job 42:7). They misapplied what God had revealed concerning Himself and His ways. Since they lacked the correct insight into the cause of Job's wretched circumstances, they did not deal wisely with him, even though they were of the opinion that they were very wise and conducted themselves very wisely.

This lack of insight manifested itself in a most painful manner for Job when they went so far as to express their doubts regarding his spiritual state and his integrity before God. Job's experiences, added to the words he uttered, were so foreign to them that they could not arrive at any other conclusion than that what they had previously heard and seen of Job had been rank hypocrisy. They reasoned that the Lord blesses those who fear Him, and that therefore a true child of God would not experience and say such things.

Job's friends are neither alone nor the last who have been guilty of not dealing wisely with those who are afflicted. And indeed, it is far from simple to behave one's self wisely toward the afflicted. This is particularly true when we encounter people who, in addition to the physical, domestic, ecclesiastical, and societal trials which all people must endure, are also tried with afflictions that are psychological in nature—trials that pertain to the mind and/or one's spiritual life. In such circumstances problems will be encountered, trials will be endured, and words will be spoken which for the inexperienced (even though they may be children or servants of God, such as Job's friends) will not only appear perplexing, but will be deemed as being incompatible with the fear of the Lord.

The results of not behaving wisely toward the afflicted are clearly described for us in the book of Job. Job clearly teaches us that even God's children can behave themselves unwisely toward the afflicted. Anyone involved with counseling will be all too familiar with this. Words can inflict wounds which neither doctors nor time can heal; only the Lord can heal them, though the scars will sometimes be evident for years. All who through the use of Scripture and professional literature are involved in the challenging work of counseling will be compelled to admit that they have made mistakes—and by the grace of God will be willing to admit it. They will readily own the words of Job and say, "Therefore have I uttered that I understood not; things too wonderful for me, which I knew not.... Wherefore I abhor myself, and repent in dust and ashes" (Job 42:3, 6). With the friends of Job, they will be more than willing to ask forgiveness of those toward whom they have behaved unwisely.

How in need we are of such grace that will prompt us to utter the humble petition, "Hear, I beseech thee, and I will speak: I will demand of thee, and declare thou unto me" (Job 42:4)!

What Is the True Cause?

The following anecdote will illustrate how important it is that the correct cause of mental distress be diagnosed by those who are called upon to interact with the person who is suffering—be it as a family member, a friend, or a professional counselor.

A member of one of the churches I have served once called upon me to help his wife. He believed his 45-year-old wife to be in great spiritual distress. When I asked him how long this had been the case, he informed me that his wife had been in this state of mind for quite some time. When I then inquired as to what he thought the cause of his wife's distress was, he responded that problems of a spiritual nature were the cause of her condition. Day and night she struggled with the question: How can I be delivered from my sin and misery?

When I went to visit this woman, I found her in bed. It was very evident that she was in great distress. I soon discovered from what she and one of her older children told me that for several days she had not left her bed. She had hardly touched her breakfast of that morning, and upon further questioning it became evident that she had hardly eaten anything for quite some time. Upon my question why she had neither left her bed nor eaten anything, she responded by saying that this made no sense since she would soon die anyway. When I asked who had told her this, she stated that her feelings told her that it was so. Reality proved, however, that her feelings had deceived her. She lived yet many years, the last of which were far better years than when I first visited her—at least as far as her spiritual life was concerned.

Believing that she was going to die and not being spiritually prepared to die caused this woman to be overcome with spiritual anxiety. It was a heart-rending experience to witness and hear what was transpiring in the life of this poor woman and her family. She did not dare to believe a word of encouragement or comfort. When she thought of God, she could only utter words of distress. For her it was true, "The thought of God brought me no peace, but rather made my fears increase; with sleepless eyes and speechless pain my fainting spirit grieved in vain; the blessedness of long ago made deeper still my present woe" (Psalter 210:2; cf. Ps. 77). Her soul refused to be comforted (Ps. 77:3), since she was convinced that there was no ground for such comfort. In her judgment she had sinned so long and so grievously; she was such a poor wife to her husband and had been such a deficient mother to her children. Thus she neither could nor dared to believe that there was one word of encouragement for her in the Bible.

During one of my many visits, I asked her husband and children whether she, as a wife and a mother, had truly failed as miserably as she claimed. They responded unanimously that they did not deem this to be the case. On the contrary, even in the church, she had the reputation of being a very devoted wife and mother who was engaged day and night on behalf of her family. Many (including myself) believed that she was a woman who truly feared the Lord—and I believe that the peaceful end of her turbulent life confirmed this. However, the fact that others believed this concerning her was of no benefit to her in the spiritual agony she was enduring. What troubled her more than anything else was that in her own estimation she was not penitent enough. She tried hard to bring herself to the point where she could feel herself to be submissive to God's justice if He would cause her to perish.

Intellectually she acquiesced in the fact that God could righteously condemn her for her sins, but she could not get her heart to do likewise. Day and night she was preoccupied with trying to bring herself to the place where she would wholeheartedly, without interruption, justify the Lord in all His doings—even though there were moments, though rare and short-lived, that she could discern within herself a bowing before God's just judgment. Her greatest agony was that she could not come to the place where she wanted to be—where she and others were convinced she had to come before there could be any change for the better.

Some sincere children of God believed that the condition of this woman was caused by the fact that the Lord was preparing her for what is referred to as "being justified in the court of one's conscience." (We understand this to mean, that in the court of conscience, a person acquires the full assurance of the pardon of his sins for the sake of the suffering and death of the Lord Jesus Christ.) They communicated this to this woman, informing her of all the things she would have to experience before this would come to pass.

She, being so desirous to acquire such assurance, fully accepted this explanation of her wretched condition, and thus she did her utmost to expedite the process. She did everything in her power to stimulate an increased sense of guilt—and she succeeded in this. This was a sign, according to her friends, that the hour of deliverance was near. These friends did everything they could to counsel her in such a manner that she would thereby be prepared for the imminent deliverance from bondage by the Word and Spirit of the Lord. They believed that this would then be the crowning piece of the work of the Lord in this woman.

She and her friends all rejected the possibility that there could be other causes contributing to her troubled state. However, the more I visited her and the more I probed to find the true cause of her condition, the more convinced I was that physical factors were contributing to her troubled state. Increasingly I felt that in addition to divine intervention this person also needed psychiatric help to be delivered from her bondage. I became convinced that the woman and her friends were mistaken in their assessment of her condition. I believed more and more that the present spiritual problems of this woman were of a psychological origin.

The woman and her friends did not share this view when I communicated it very cautiously to them. This greatly hindered me in the pastoral care I sought to provide. In spite of all the care this woman received, her condition deteriorated. She spent most of her time in bed. This obviously resulted in a very stressful situation for her family. When I suggested that her physician should be consulted, I encountered much resistance. She insisted that the doctor could not make her better, for he would not be able to deliver her from her sins. Only the Lord could do this. She insisted, "I am not sick; I am only concerned because of my sins. Only the Lord can help me. It is only because of my spiritual problems that I am so miserable. When I am delivered from them, everything will be solved and I will be better. Perhaps the doctor will prescribe medication that will make me drowsy. Perhaps he will send me to a psychiatrist and from there to a psychiatric hospital. I do not want that. This is not necessary, and I may not do it, for then I would turn to man for deliverance. I will persevere in prayer and the reading of the Bible."

Several weeks transpired before I finally decided to take action. I gave her family the opportunity to seek the intervention of their physician before 5:00 p.m. on a given day. I informed her that if her family would fail to do so, then I would step in. I told her that before God I would take full responsibility for this decision—and thus neither she nor her husband would be responsible. If things were to turn out wrong, I would bear the consequences.

To my great joy, the husband informed me that night that he had contacted the doctor. He in turn referred her to a Christian psychiatrist, and the following day already, the woman received the medication she needed for the restoration of her health. She was not admitted to a psychiatric hospital, and slowly but surely her spiritual concerns were reduced to normal proportions. The Lord gave deliverance—but with measure and in an entirely different manner than this woman and others had anticipated.

I am still of the opinion that the problems this woman encountered were related to hormonal changes (she was approximately 45 years of age). It is a known fact that hormonal changes in the body can precipitate serious mental distress. I was pleased when I recently heard from a medical professor that within medical circles there is a growing consensus that not only women but also men may experience such a period of transition during this time of life.

When we are subjected to mental stress, our religious experiences will be affected accordingly. When our mental condition is such that we can no longer deal with life's problems in a normal fashion, we will also not be able to deal normally with matters pertaining to our spiritual well-being. There will then be neurotic feelings of guilt and anxiety which do not proceed from God, but from our mental state. Such feelings require a different approach than normal convictions of sin, righteousness, and judgment, which are the fruit of the saving ministry of the Holy Spirit.

Can the convicting ministry of the Holy Spirit in the

heart of a believer be accompanied by clinical symptoms of mental distress? Most certainly! Having said that, it is entirely wrong to relegate all concern about guilt and sin to the category of mental disturbances. First of all, this is not true, and secondly, this is not the way to counsel those who are troubled because of their sins. Experience teaches us that the Lord frequently uses times of stress and illness, also those of a psychological nature, to lead sinners in the way of righteousness. The experience of having to surrender fully because we can no longer govern the rudder of our lives can be very healthy for us. We have to learn that we cannot force God's hand. It is only in the way of following Him that we are made wise unto salvation in this present life, as well as for the life to come. Our sinful nature often prescribes to the Lord what He must do, and when and how He must do it.

The Lord taught us to pray, "Thy will be done." How we need to pray this petition every day of our lives—yes, every moment of the day! With the Lord there is much forgiveness (also for our sin of wanting to be in control) through the blood of Him who became a Servant though He was Lord, and who placed God's will above His own when He said, "Not my will, but thy will be done." The Lord has also provided the grace to enable us to follow Him—even in the most grievous circumstances—so that we may experience that "all those who fear and trust His name...no want shall know" (Psalter 87:2).

The Lord also granted this to the woman whose story I have just related. In addition to being healed in mind and body, the Lord granted her spiritual deliverance. The circumstances in which she found herself worked together for her good, albeit in a different manner than she had anticipated.

No one ought to aspire after the experience of grievous bondage. Instead, we should desire clarity and genuineness. If the latter should be accompanied with some measure of difficulty and bondage, no one should use this as a benchmark to determine whether such experiences are of a saving nature. At all times let us seek the Lord's countenance until for Jesus' sake He will be gracious to us, leaving the manner and measure in which He deals with us to be determined by His wisdom, sovereignty, righteousness, and mercy. Without the ministry of the Holy Spirit it is impossible to submit to this. However, the Lord is pleased when we call upon Him for this grace. "If ye then, being evil, know how to give good gifts unto your children: how much more shall your heavenly Father give the Holy Spirit to them that ask him?" (Luke 11:13). These are the words of the Savior. Therefore,

> While He proffers peace and pardon,
> Let us hear His voice today,
> Lest if we our hearts should harden,
> We should perish in the way.
> —Psalter 255:4

—3—
Lonely and Miserable

In this article we will return to the history recorded in 1 Kings 19. We should be grateful to the Lord that He has caused the circumstances preceding Elijah's depression to be recorded. Since everything in the Bible has been recorded for our instruction, it will be to our benefit to pay close attention to every detail and to examine it within the total context of what has been revealed to us in God's Word. Especially the latter we may not forget to do, since we could then readily be guilty of extracting something from the text that the Lord has not put in it. This will also safeguard us against thinking that a given passage of Scripture is applicable only to a given person and/or his circumstances—and then reasoning that since I am not that person, it is not applicable to me. By such reasoning we will deprive ourselves of much that could be to our benefit. How often this occurs, especially with people who are suffering from depression! Since their mental condition is such that their mental capacities do not function normally, they respond inappropriately to everything they are called upon to believe. They neither can nor dare to believe what both

God and people are saying to them, even though they would very much desire to.

There is a significant and essential difference between the unbelief of someone who is mentally strong and healthy, and that of people who for various reasons are mentally weak or ill. Whoever loses sight of this will be inconsiderate in his judgment of himself and others. The Lord will not judge us in such a fashion; His justice is not the justice of a judge who, void of feeling, has no regard for the circumstances at hand. The Lord judges and punishes righteously—that is, in proportion to the measure in which a person can be held accountable for his actions and reactions.

Those who divorce Elijah's flight from Jezreel, after having received Jezebel's message, from all that preceded this (as explained earlier) will misjudge his flight and what followed. We have seen that the misjudgment of someone's circumstances can have serious consequences for the person himself as well as for others. Misjudgment can greatly aggravate the depression of one who is "fleeing"—one who is "afflicted, tossed with tempest, and not comforted" (Isa. 54:11)—along with all the wretched consequences. When verbiage such as "exaggeration," "acting like a child," and "this is your own fault" is used in response to genuine phobias, the depression will only become worse.

When someone suffers from serious fatigue (either mentally or physically), he will process things very differently from when he is not fatigued. This is entirely normal. However, a state of excessive fatigue can lead to total exhaustion. When a situation arises in which a person is both mentally and physically exhausted (as was true for Elijah), he can then readily be overcome with a sense of panic when dramatic events take place. This can happen even when rather insignificant events occur.

When Jezebel swore that she would see to it that the next day would be his last, Elijah did not respond by saying, "The Lord is God; my times are in His hands." Instead, Elijah flees—apparently without having asked, "Lord, what wilt Thou have me to do?" Only shortly before, his strong faith in his God had prompted him to speak and act boldly. None of this was exhibited now. Elijah, who we would have thought feared no one when he confronted Ahab and slew the very priests of Baal who had been honored and preserved by Ahab and his wife— now fled for fear of Jezebel's revenge. The man whose heart only shortly before had been overflowing with a goodly theme and who with an eager tongue and joyful song had praised the King divine (Psalter 124:1), was now filled with anxiety and fear after receiving Jezebel's message. The spiritual eye of Elijah that had been fixed so steadfastly upon the invisible God when he carried out his task could now only see Jezebel and death. Elijah did not say what, centuries later, the godly Elector Frederick III of the Paltz said when one tried to prevent him from attending the Diet of Augsburg in 1566 where he had to appear in connection with the publication of the Heidelberg Catechism. The Elector said that if they wanted to take his life, they would only shorten the time before he would enter eternal glory!

The conduct of the Elector shows us what is possible by the grace of God. This was also evident in Elijah's conduct prior to his flight. The fact that Elijah fled, and the manner in which did so, confirm that he remained a man of like passions as we are. The confession, "The Lord is with me; I shall not fear" and being filled with fear can be in such close proximity to each other—even in the life of those who are most exercised and advanced in grace!

To be able to believe, one not only needs the grace of the Holy Spirit, but also God-given mental capacities to respond in faith to whatever befalls us. To properly handle a message such as Jezebel's, one needs a significant measure of mental fortitude. Elijah evidently did not have this when he received her message.

One might ask, "Why did not the Lord give Elijah the mental fortitude he so very much needed?" My response is, "Who can stay his hand, or say unto him, 'What doest thou?'" (Dan. 4:35). God's ways are higher than our ways. It must obviously have been for Elijah's edification and salvation—and that of many others—and thus to God's honor that he experienced the things recorded for us in the Bible. "All things work together for good to those that love God" (Rom. 8:28). Only afterwards will this be acknowledged by all whom the Lord called according to His purpose and exercised in the most holy faith. By God's goodness and grace, many who thought that something strange befell them have been encouraged by Elijah's experience. For Elijah, this experience also proceeded from the fatherly hands of God. Those hands will not spare flesh and blood when we must learn lessons that will be subservient to God's honor, our salvation, and the salvation of others.

As can be deduced from 1 Kings 18 and 19, Elijah's request to die and his lying down beneath the juniper tree were preceded by a period of great anxiety, unsettledness, and restlessness.

Upon consulting the map of the land of Palestine, one will discover that the distance between Jezreel and Beersheba is rather significant for someone who must travel on foot. Jezreel is located in the northern part of the country, whereas Beersheba is located in the south. We are not told how long it took Elijah to travel from Jezreel to Beersheba. We can readily imagine that Elijah did not rest very often as he was fleeing. When we feel threatened by danger, it is not easy to find a place to rest or even find the time to rest. When we are no longer in control of our situation, whatever the reason may be, stopping what we are doing is simply no longer possible, regardless of how tired or exhausted we may be. The strength is lacking to keep our thoughts and heart from racing. In some situations, sedatives can then be helpful in regaining one's composure. However, when more than composure is needed to process everything normally, also such means will not have the desired effect.

Perilous Solitude

During his flight from Jezreel to Beersheba, Elijah was accompanied by his helper. In Beersheba, Elijah communicated to this young man that he should stay there. Elijah wanted to travel alone; the company of the boy was too much for him. Elijah may have been of the opinion that solitude would be better for him. In reality, however, his separation from his helper—the last of Elijah's confidantes—became a contributing factor in Elijah's descent into the abyss from which he cried out, "It is enough; now, O LORD, take away my life; for I am not better than my fathers" (1 Kings 19:4).

People whose depression becomes serious often begin to withdraw themselves from everything and everyone. They insist on being alone as they dwell on their problems, reflecting on ways and means which could lead to deliverance from their anxiety and problems. The conversation of others, even of those with whom they have enjoyed the most friendly and intimate relationships, is a burden to them. Since they are so preoccupied with themselves, everything and everyone else lose their significance. By isolating themselves they cause much grief to those who are nearest to them, and they also render themselves a great disservice. To withdraw from family during a period of mental exhaustion and despondency is perilous indeed! Solomon said that "two are better than one" (Eccl. 4:9).

What must it have been for Elijah's helper when his master informed him that he wanted to proceed without him into the wilderness! This young man, who undoubtedly perceived that Elijah was in great straits, wanted to do everything he could to assist his master, and yet knew that there was nothing he could do for Elijah! This young man was in a position where his only option was to let Elijah continue without him, however troubling this must have been to him.

We must do everything in our power to prevent depressed individuals from withdrawing themselves into isolation. When confronted with such a situation, we should simply refuse to grant them their wish. At that moment the person who wishes to be left alone will not appreciate this.

It is in the best interest of the depressed person that he is surrounded by people who know him. I know all too well from experience that I did not want to interact with anybody when I suffered from the depression of which I have written in *A Helping Hand*. I am now grateful to those who refused to leave me alone. Their presence and commitment were of greater benefit to me than I recognized at that time. It is painful for spouses, children, or friends when they notice that their presence is not appreciated by those who are depressed. However, this will also turn for the better once recovery takes place.

At times it simply cannot be prevented that depressed persons go into the "wilderness." That will leave us with but one option: To pray to God to whom belong the issues of death (Ps. 68:20). At such times faith in a God who hears and answers prayer will be greatly tested. These are times when not only in the heart of the depressed person but also in the heart of all who prayerfully seek to assist and guide, the "voice" will be heard, "Where is thy God?" (Ps. 42:10). What fearful nights depressed people then have to endure, as well as those who desire nothing less than their recovery! We read in Psalm 145:18, "The LORD is nigh unto all them that call upon him"—and this is indeed true. Countless people have found this to be true. There are, however, also countless people who concur with the poet of Psalm 73, "But as for me, my feet were almost gone; my steps had well nigh slipped" (v. 2).

The Lord was also near to a lonely Elijah traveling into the wilderness—an Elijah who was tossed with tempest. Had that not been true, Elijah would have perished in the wilderness.

The faithful covenant-keeping Jehovah will not leave such souls to fend for themselves who in their "better" days feared Him, called upon His Name, submitted to His rule, and looked to Him for help. The praying High Priest in heaven also prays for them during seasons when they are neither able nor dare to pray—and who, due to their circumstances for a season do not even want to pray. How important it therefore is to remember the Lord Jehovah before the evil days come!

The Lord will show His mercy toward those for whom such evil days are the first occasion of humbling themselves under the mighty hand of God until He would also be merciful to them for Jesus' sake. For His Name and covenant's sake, the Lord will also be gracious to those who, in their sins and misery, turn to Him for deliverance. "He will regard the prayer of the destitute, and not despise their prayer" (Ps. 102:17).

Wrong Notions

In his book *An Answer to Depression*, Norman Wright states: "Elijah is a classic example of a man who suffered as a result of depression. As a result of his despair he wanted to die. He entertained wrong notions about him-self, others, and God." I wish to pursue this a bit further.

Elijah's statement, "I am no better than my fathers," can be interpreted in various ways. When we consider this statement in light of Elijah's circumstances, then I believe that Norman Wright is correct that Elijah entertained wrong notions concerning himself.

It is well-known that depressed persons entertain very low thoughts of themselves and the work they have accom-plished during their lifetimes. It can be a fruit of God's grace when we have low thoughts of ourselves and our work. Humility is a fruit of the Spirit, and the more hum-ble a person is, the better. However, we must neither confuse nor equate the humility which is a fruit of the Spirit with the opinion a depressed person has of himself and his accomplishments.

A depressed person will think and say, "I am an utterly worthless individual; I have never accomplished anything. I am a failure and good-for-nothing; I occupy an utterly useless place upon this globe. I am a misfit, and I don't know how to do anything right." Respect and confidence for God's gifts have both vanished and have been replaced by self-denunciation.

Sometimes such a depressed state of mind is caused by people. If all we ever hear is how we have failed and come short, we will begin to feel inferior about ourselves, and such feelings can readily culminate in depression.

Sometimes we ourselves are to be blamed for being very despondent by constantly downgrading ourselves and our accomplishments. Instead of accepting ourselves with our limitations, including the fact that we are and will remain sinners who must seek our righteousness out-side of ourselves in the Lord Jesus Christ, we will bombard ourselves with all manner of self-denunciation. This is not good!

Sparrows and Nightingales

In the world of birds, God has created both sparrows and nightingales. In comparison to the small number of nightingales, there are many sparrows. Is that a deficiency in God's creation? I do not believe so. Likewise, if we belong to the many "sparrows" God has created among the children of men, preserving them as such, do we then not shortchange God and ourselves if we consider only the "nightingales" to be people of worth, and thus consider ourselves of little or no worth? It is a form of pride when we cannot accept ourselves as a "sparrow" and are dissatisfied with the fact that we are not a "nightingale," wishing to be, or to appear to be, more than we are. We thereby grieve the Lord and make ourselves miserable. God does not require a sparrow to sing like a nightingale. Let us therefore not demand of ourselves what we see others accomplish but cannot accomplish ourselves due to the fact that we are simply not like them.

Acceptance of God's gifts leads to self-respect, self-confidence, and gratitude. Self-acceptance is therefore God-glorifying and pleasing to Him. It yields rest and joy in being engaged in the task committed and entrusted to us, even though we may not excel beyond others in certain accomplishments.

It is wrong to pat ourselves on the back when something has been accomplished as a result of our initiative. It is equally wrong, however, to focus on what we have not accomplished. In 1 Corinthians 15:10 we have a clear example of humility accompanied with a healthy opinion of one's accomplishments: "But by the grace of God I am what I am: and his grace which was bestowed upon me was not in vain; but I laboured more abundantly than they all: yet not I, but the grace of God which was with me." Paul knew very well that he daily offended in many things (James 3:2; cf. Rom. 7; Phil. 3:12), and yet he did not go so far as to cast out all his accomplishments. I do not believe that this is God's will. In contrast to sinful forms of self-confidence and self-respect, there are also those that are good, necessary, and useful. Without a healthy sense of these, human beings cannot function well. We may pray for an appropriate sense of self-confidence and self-respect, clothed in true humility, and we must oppose everything that impedes a healthy development of these things (be it in ourselves or others) with the Word of God. True humility will manifest itself when the Holy Spirit applies the Word of God to our hearts.

Insufficient Lighting

In situations such as Elijah's, Satan, the murderer from the beginning, is often very active. He knows where, when, and how we have failed. He will take advantage of this to increase our despondency—and, if possible, lead us to despair. He will point to our "filthy garments" (Zech. 3:4) without directing us to the blood of Jesus Christ, God's Son, which cleanses from all sin (1 John 1:7).

Quite possibly, Satan also assaulted Elijah during his flight with questions such as, "Where is your faith that God reigns? The fact that you are fleeing proves that you believe that Jezebel reigns! Are you not the greatest hypocrite that ever lived? There is no harmony between your words and your deeds. Your walk of life does not agree with your profession. Should you not have remained in Jezreel? Should you not have remained with those who need your help so much?"

In everyone's life there are things which will press down our shoulders and cause us to cast down our eyes when reminded of them. When we are conscious of our sins and failures without this being countered by what we read in Zechariah 3:2, "The LORD rebuke thee, O Satan; even the LORD that hath chosen Jerusalem rebuke thee," then nothing will remain for us but to agree with those voices within. When I have no rebuttal for my accusers and must agree that I am a deserter, that I have come short in everything, that I am a failure, that I have ruined everything—this will make me choose death above life.

From the world of photography we know that if there is insufficient lighting when an object is photographed, the photograph will look much darker than reality. One of Satan's tactics with depressed people is to present things in such a fashion that everything appears to be much darker than it is in reality. What a blessed fact that the Son of God has been manifested to destroy the works of the devil! Satan can do much, but he cannot do everything.

To be delivered from depression, Elijah not only needed a fresh supply of physical and mental energy, but he also needed instruction. Instruction not only cured his wrong notions regarding himself, but he also had to be cured of his wrong notions regarding the fruit of his work among his people and the ways of the Lord. By His light, the Lord will cause us to see things the way they really are. How good and upright is the LORD in teaching sinners in the way, guiding them in judgment and teaching them His way (Ps. 25:8-9)!

Elijah's opinion that he was not better than his fathers was not the fruit of Spirit-wrought self-knowledge. This view of himself was a distortion, resulting from physical and mental exhaustion, as well as his brooding during his fleeing from Jezebel.

Elijah's petition to be allowed to die did not proceed from the Spirit either, but rather, from his flesh. He was battle-weary, and weary of life itself.

The Lord neither granted Elijah his request nor caused him to perish in his misery. By His providential arrangement and instruction, He delivered Elijah from all his difficulties and gave him new courage and desire to live. This has been recorded for our instruction, so that we too, in the midst of all our difficulties, would continue to flee to the throne of grace for help in time of need. The Lord will chastise us, but never commensurate to our sins. At His time and in His way, the Lord will heal the broken-hearted for the sake of His Son and His Name.

— 4 —
Satan's Devices

Depressed individuals are frequently of the opinion that they have committed the unpardonable sin. It will therefore be useful to focus on this.

A few years ago someone rang the doorbell at our parsonage. A man of about thirty years of age stood before me, in great distress. When I asked him what troubled him, he responded that he was beside himself because of his sins. Upon my request to tell me more about this sensitive matter, he informed me that he believed he had sinned against the Holy Ghost.

From literature I have read, as well as from personal experience, I know that there are many people who are fearful of having committed this sin. The Lord Jesus said concerning this sin in Matthew 12:31-33, "Wherefore I say unto you, All manner of sin and blasphemy shall be forgiven unto men: but the blasphemy against the Holy Ghost shall not be forgiven unto men. And whosoever speaketh a word against the Son of man, it shall be forgiven him: but whosoever speaketh against the Holy Ghost, it shall not be forgiven him, neither in this world, neither in the world to come."

The Sin Against the Holy Ghost
People who for a variety of reasons have become mentally

unstable or who suffer from mental illness are frequently troubled and tormented by the thought of having sinned against the Holy Ghost. A number of those who are troubled about this will verbalize their anxiety. Others (probably a far larger number) remain silent about what the true cause of their anxiety is. It is easy to understand that people would rather not speak about this, for this sin is the most dreadful sin a person can commit. Such people know that upon admitting that they have committed this sin, they will be asked to explain why they believe this to be the case. This would mean that they would have to speak about those sins of which they are so deeply ashamed.

Numerous times during my pastoral career I have been asked by people of all ages what it means to have sinned against the Holy Ghost. In many cases it became evident to me that this question was triggered by an unexpressed fear one had committed this sin. Many have made a diligent effort to answer this question. Frequently such troubled souls can be told that they most certainly have not committed this sin. Whether they will believe this is another issue. The fear of having committed this sin will stubbornly persist— particularly when an individual is either depressed or is suffering from a nervous breakdown.

Upon asking such troubled souls what constitutes the sin against the Holy Ghost, it is not uncommon to get the response, "I do not know." Others will often respond by saying that they have repeatedly sinned against God's commandments, and that they have done so against better knowledge, as a result of which they now perceive a great hardness of heart. They draw the conclusion then that they have committed the unpardonable sin. There is also the common notion that this sin consists in having ignored God's callings and in having resisted the inner stirrings of the conscience when God's callings came to them. When people are of the opinion that they have committed the unpardonable sin because they have so grievously and frequently sinned against God's commandments, then we must tell them that such is not the case. When we transgress the Lord's commandments, we do indeed resist and grieve the Spirit. When one hardens himself in response to the callings of the Lord and the inner stirrings triggered by them, he will be guilty of quenching the Spirit. However, the unpardonable sin of slandering and blaspheming the Spirit is a different matter. In committing this sin, one does not sin against the commandments of God, but rather, against the divine Persons. This sin is also not committed due to either ignorance or weakness, but it is committed with malicious intent. It is a speaking against the Holy Ghost which is evil in nature—only consider the meaning of the word "to slander." This sin is therefore a premeditated, conscious, calculated, and intentional act of calling the work of the Holy Ghost the work of the devil.

Only consider the context in which the Lord Jesus expressed the words found in Matthew 12:31-32. The neglect, due to either ignorance or inattentiveness, of considering the context in which God's declarations occur in His Word, is an important cause of much misery. One of the specialties of the prince of darkness is to take portions of God's Word out of their context. He is highly skilled in this art. He will change the truth into a half truth. This is something the liar from the beginning delights to do in order to bring people to despair—to cause them to believe that there is no forgiveness for them. He will then get them to believe that it now no longer makes any sense to pray, read, or go to church. Or he will seek to persuade them that it is better to commit suicide—or to yield fully to those sins that are so attractive to the flesh, enjoying life a little.

Oh, the devices of Satan are many! What need we have time and again and under all circumstances to pray, "Order my steps in thy word: and let not any iniquity have dominion over me" (Ps. 119:133).

The Son of God has been manifested to destroy the works of the devil. He is the only One who can and will do this to all who, in the midst of their troubles, continue to make supplication at the throne of God.

The sins over which we grieve are pardonable not because we grieve sufficiently over them with sufficient repentance, but because the blood of Jesus Christ, God's Son, cleanses from all sin (1 John 1:8). He who grieves over the things he has either said or done, thinking that he has consequently sinned against the Holy Ghost, has the proof within himself that he has not committed this sin. No one will ever grieve over that sin. They who have committed this sin did so consciously, deliberately, and with malicious delight—they will never regret it. They will neither ask nor seek forgiveness for this sin.

If a person does not know what it means to blaspheme the Spirit, he needs to be instructed that one cannot commit this sin ignorantly. In fact, would a sin committed in ignorance, without knowing what one either said or did or what it means to commit that sin, be unpardonable with the Lord? That is impossible! This is precluded in light of what the Bible teaches us regarding God's justice and mercy. First Timothy 1:13 yields the proof for this. The Holy Spirit inspired Paul to write the following for our instruction: "Who was before a blasphemer, and a persecutor, and injurious: but I obtained mercy, because I did it ignorantly in unbelief." What a blessing it is that this is also recorded in the Bible!

Illusion and Reality
Why is it that people who have not committed the sin

against the Holy Ghost—who could not have committed it—are so troubled that they have committed this sin? Since they are either fearful or convinced of having committed this sin, we must, for the sake of their well-being, deal with this problem more in depth. Many have occupied themselves with this question and its answer.

Is it possible that the Holy Spirit Himself convinced such people of having committed this sin? No, this cannot be the case. We read concerning the Holy Spirit in John 16:8-9, "And when he is come, he will reprove the world of sin, and of righteousness, and of judgment: of sin, because they believe not on me." Here we observe that the Holy Spirit does not reprove of the sin of having blasphemed Him. The fear or conviction of having sinned against the Holy Ghost is not the fruit of His work. From whence then does this proceed?

In the first place the evil spirit, Satan, suggests to people that they have committed this sin. People who have unburdened themselves to me in this regard have frequently told me that they could not explain why such thoughts would repeatedly occur to them. The liar and murderer from the beginning, who due to his observation and experience of many centuries has a keen knowledge of human nature, is an expert in deluding and deceiving people. He has everything to gain by persuading people that they have committed the unpardonable sin. A deep sense of despair is fruitful soil for the development of the seeds of sin which are concealed in our hearts. The great enemy of man's happiness and salvation, Satan, is continually looking for an opportunity to destroy whomever he can—either as an angel of light or as a roaring lion.

To accomplish this, he makes use—or rather he abuses—the various circumstances of life. The weaker and more unstable one's state of mind is, the better his chances of success are—that is, insofar as the Lord permits according to His just and wise government. This explains why people who are mentally unstable or ill so frequently suffer from the thought of having committed the unpardonable sin.

It is well-known that those who, at a time when they suffered from either mental instability or mental illness, were oppressed with the fear of having sinned against the Holy Ghost, were almost imperceptibly delivered from that fear upon recovering mentally. If, however, they experience another dip (which occurs rather frequently since the mentally afflicted usually recover with ups and downs), then their former fear frequently surfaces again. Excessive stress will cause one to sink through it into the previously experienced misery. The only thing that remains for those who suffer or who counsel them is to prayerfully cast our burden upon Him who said, "Call upon me in the day of trouble: I will deliver thee, and thou shalt glorify me" (Ps. 50:15), doing so until He will once more be gracious to us.

In addition to Satan, our own minds can at times be the cause of fear of having committed the unpardonable sin. It is "normal" for a person whose mind is troubled, disturbed, weak, or ill, to be of a very restless disposition and to search for the cause of this restlessness. For someone with a religious training, the cause appears to be obvious: my sins are the cause.

This searching for an explanation for the misery frequently leads to a conscious or unconscious fostering of feelings of guilt. If this disposition does not change as a result of the Holy Spirit's application of the instruction of the Holy Scriptures, a man will be inclined to formulate his own explanation for the misery he is in. He will then diagnose his own condition and thereby tell himself and others what the cause of his misery is. Being in such a condition, it is quite common that the thoughts of the oppressed and troubled person will become obsessed with thoughts such as these: "Did I commit the unpardonable sin? My heart is so hard; my thoughts are so wrong; nothing appeals to me anymore; I cannot believe anything anymore; I am no longer interested in anything; I believe that I have been given over to total hardness; I believe that I have committed the unpardonable sin."

When these thoughts become embedded in an unstable mind, they often lead to the conclusion: "Now I am sure of it! I must have committed that sin, or else my condition would be entirely different."

Such a person can neither see nor believe that he has unconsciously maneuvered himself into a corner in which only this awful conclusion remains. He arrives at such a conclusion because he reasoned with his own feelings and opinion rather than with the Holy Scriptures. As a result of being mentally afflicted, the emotions and the will do not function normally—in fact, cannot function normally. This means that one's feelings and perceptions will be about the worst compass to use in such circumstances.

Since the unity of the human body is such that when one member suffers, all the members suffer, such mental malaise will, in addition to one's emotions and will, also affect the mind. Such a person is not crazy, but rather, confused and often terribly tired from all this brooding. All of this is detrimental to the proper processing of life's problems.

The mind could also not be functioning properly in these circumstances due to the use of medications that cause drowsiness. The physician may deem it necessary to prescribe such medications, the use of which may not be neglected. Never may we regulate the use of prescribed medications without consulting the physician who is treating us. We thereby endanger our well-being. We will have to accept the side-effects of certain medications, as our physician must at times choose the lesser of two evils to facilitate our healing.

When in addition to our emotions and our will, our mind does not function normally (as is true in the situations we have just described), we will be more or less compelled to move about in a circle that becomes ever smaller, robbing us of the desire and courage to live.

A hopeless case? No! The afflicted person will view himself as such, and the one who counsels him may think likewise. But, thanks be to God! For a Triune God, for the Savior Jesus Christ, it is not a hopeless case! That is the testimony of God's Word, confirmed by the experience of many who by God's grace and goodness have been brought up out of the horrible pit and the miry clay (Ps. 40:2).

There is a great difference between thinking we have committed a sin and knowing we committed a sin. Those whose minds are not functioning normally due to either weakness or illness are particularly vulnerable to such illusions. An illusion is something we imagine to be true, but which is not substantiated by facts.

Such illusions are frequently related to a previous experience, or to something one feels at the moment—something that we label and upon which we base our conclusion. People who suffer from such illusions are greatly troubled. They are first of all troubled because they are completely convinced that what they imagine is true. They are furthermore troubled because no one but the Lord can deliver them from such an illusion. As long as their mental state does not improve nor change, no one will be able to change their mind about such illusions. It is impossible to deal rationally with such illusions.

Obviously this does not mean that we should refrain from speaking to a person who suffers from such illusions, simply because we cannot reason with him. That is not at all the case! We must indeed dialog with such a person, so that he will not become more isolated and sink even more deeply into the pit of misery. In conversations with such individuals, an effort must be made to ascertain what is the cause of such illusions. They can be symptomatic of the disease—symptomatic of those who are either burnt out and/or depressed. It is far from easy to deal and live with people who suffer these problems.

Such illusions can vary in nature. When they are of a religious nature, we will need divine light to be able to distinguish illusion from reality. Who can determine whether someone is suffering from imaginary or real problems? The one who is in distress will certainly not be able to do so. He will not be able to evaluate his thoughts objectively. A competent counselor will have to do this—and not everyone who presents himself as such, or is esteemed to be such, is competent in this area.

Before turning to a professional counselor—be it a doctor, psychologist, psychiatrist, or whoever else may have been professionally trained to give therapy—it first needs to be investigated whether such an individual is competent to render assistance in specific cases. A recommendation from within one's own immediate circle of family and friends can be very significant in such a situation.

Quite often we must regretfully come to the conclusion that even those who have been professionally trained to give therapy (especially in the realm of psychiatry) cause those from our own circles who are entrusted to them to be more anxious rather than to find relief. It is a most formidable challenge to deal with those whose illusions pertain to matters of religion.

A child of God does not necessarily have the expertise to give appropriate counsel to people who have problems of a religious nature. Even though he or she may have learned either by the Holy Spirit's teaching or by experience to distinguish between illusion and reality, this does not mean that they are therefore the most suitable person to counsel people who are mentally distressed. Believers can utter words that inflict such deep spiritual wounds that they are beyond the realm of human restoration. This will particularly be true when such words are uttered by one whose judgment we value because he is deemed to be either a child or servant of the Lord. Ministers, elders, and deacons must therefore be very careful in such situations. In difficult cases, they ought to seek the counsel of those who are knowledgeable and experienced in this area. Let them practice self-denial by referring such troubled souls (upon mutual consultation and concurrence) to someone they believe will be more capable than themselves.

Above all, we should not forget as either patient or counselor to seek the help of Him who is mighty to save. By His Word and Spirit, He can furnish solutions and bring about deliverance, also from illusions. He can do so even in cases where we find ourselves utterly helpless to render assistance or to rid ourselves of our illusions.

The Lord will indeed be merciful to those who humbly seek Him—who in the midst of all their trouble continue to turn to God's throne, and in spite of all setbacks, continue to hope in His goodness (cf. Psalms 145 and 147). However hopeless everything may appear to be—yes, even when you utter groan upon groan when thinking about God (cf. Psalms 77 and 86)—do not cease to lift up your heart and eyes on high for yourself and others. I know what it is to be in such circumstances—to hope against hope and to believe that there will yet be deliverance. I know how impossible it is in our own strength to continue to hope in God in the face of the most discouraging circumstances—yes, how foolish it often seems. Thanks be to God, I also know that the Lord is a God who performs miracles. Miracles are those phenomena for which no one can give a scientific explanation. God can work such miracles without the use of means, or some-times by way of people, medication, and rest.

If we really desire to help those in distress, we must first of all learn to listen. This is exceptionally difficult, es-pecially when such individuals cannot or will not say anything about the cause of their distress. Then we must very carefully seek to draw them out. This takes time, de-mands patience, and necessitates prayer.

When I fully listened to the man who feared that he had committed the unpardonable sin, I was convinced that this was an illusion. I obviously endeavored to con-vince him of this, but in vain. I also discussed other matters with him about which he was most surprised.

One of the things that surprised him was that I asked him whether he had recently been working much over-time. I could read in his face that he thought, "What does this have to do with my spiritual problems?" With some hesitation, the man admitted that for quite some time he had worked many extra hours. Consequently, he had fre-quently gone to bed late and had gotten little sleep, having to be at work early the next morning.

When I advised him to visit his family doctor to find ways and means to recover from the physical and mental exhaustion caused by his lifestyle, he was speechless for a moment. He looked at me with amazement, saying after a few moments, "But pastor, you are the one who must help me with my problems rather than my doctor! Only the Lord is able to help me. My sins are the cause of my mis-ery rather than my work!" After having calmed and reassured him that he had done the right thing in coming to me with his problems—being the first in line, as his shepherd, to help him in his need—I told him why he should go to the doctor. I was convinced that the spiritual distress of this man was related to physical problems.

If for a sustained period of time we are guilty of abusing our bodies, our minds, or both, we will have to deal with the consequences. This will manifest itself sooner at times with one person than with another, the reason being, that one person will be stronger in mind and/or spirit than the other. No one can sin against his body without consequences. This is true first of all because our body is in need of diligent care in order to function well. This is true in all areas of life. If someone neglects his car and fails to secure timely maintenance, he should not be surprised when on a given day, at a most inopportune and unexpected moment, he will have difficulties. Would then our body, this complex masterpiece of God's creation in which every component of the body and the mind are interdependent in such a harmonious manner, not be in need of diligent care?

Secondly, one cannot continue to sin against his body without consequences, since this renders us guilty before God who calls us to be stewards of our bodies and minds by using them in a proper fashion.

It is, of course, possible that one can become exhausted without being guilty of such things. I am thinking of exhaustion as a result of illness, pregnancies, miscarriages, difficulty in giving birth, etc.

Whether someone's troubles during a certain period of difficulty are directly and objectively connected to a committed sin, is a matter which the distressed or depressed person cannot judge. When one is in such a state, he will be vulnerable to the illusion of having committed certain sins.

When we are troubled about sin because of our state of mind, such troubles will vanish in proportion to the improvement of our mental state. Being troubled about sin as a result of the ministry of the Holy Spirit will not be relieved until we, by faith, humbly take refuge to the blood of Christ, which is also a fruit of the Holy Spirit. Since the

Lord has also provided medications which can be sub-servient to the healing of our mind, we should consult our physicians in situations in which our trouble about sin is neurotic in nature. To properly digest matters of a reli-gious nature, we need a healthy mind. It is therefore my opinion that it is the Lord's will that we use prescribed medication that facilitates the healing of our mind. When the Lord is pleased to bless such means, using His Word at the same time unto our salvation, our neurotic distress will vanish and a healthy concern about truly committed sins will remain. At the time and manner of God's choos-ing this will lead to the experience of God's salvation as articulated, for example, in Psalm 32.

One will later thank God for having led us in such a way to the knowledge of salvation. In that way we learned to distinguish between illusion and reality. The disappear-ance of such neurotic distress and the remaining of a healthy concern about sin is something I have observed in myself as well as others.

This was, for instance, also the case with the man whose experiences I have just described. After he had con-sulted his physician, had for some time taken some appropriate medication, and had enjoyed an extra meas-ure of rest, his concern about having sinned against the Holy Ghost vanished slowly but surely. Subsequent to this I never heard him speak of this again.

If one experiences something of what David experi-enced in Psalm 32:3-4, it will certainly have an effect upon our psychological condition. We read there, "When I kept silence, my bones waxed old through my roaring all the day long. For day and night thy hand was heavy upon me: my moisture is turned into the drought of summer."

In Psalm 51:5, we read about the same period in David's life: "For I acknowledge my transgressions: and my sin is ever before me." It should be obvious to all that he is not referring here to sins he imagined to have committed, but to sins he knew that he had committed.

When one is weighed down by this sense of guilt, being bowed down by the crushing accusations of an accusing and condemning law, an accusing conscience, to which the accuser of the brethren, Satan, joins himself, this will not fail to leave deep furrows in the psyche of such an individual. When such an experience is long in duration, it can cause a serious mental disturbance, along with all the misery that accompanies it.

The Bible makes clear that Satan will make use of all the vicissitudes of a person's life. When did Satan approach Jesus with his temptations? It was after He had fasted for forty days and forty nights. It is self-evident that He who was truly man had become weak as a result of this lengthy fast. Satan could make no inroads upon Christ, but he can do so with us, especially when we are physically and/or mentally exhausted. Happily the Lord restricts Satan in his activities in which he aims to seduce and destroy us, or else no one would be saved.

Heredity can also contribute significantly to the occurrence of depressions. When depressions frequently occur in someone's family, we refer to such a person as being genetically predisposed. One ought not to think, however, that if there is a frequent occurrence of depression in his family, that he will be afflicted likewise—and thus become a patient himself. That is not necessarily the case! In fact, when one senses himself becoming depressed, it can be profitable to think, "No wonder, this is part of our family profile." This makes it possible to face this issue much more calmly.

Experience also teaches us that things can be so different from day to day. Things can look so much brighter, just as this is true for the weather. Even the difference in weather can make a significant difference as to whether we are more or less depressed.

By way of such logical deductions much anxiety regarding this can be prevented. Instead, it can help us to relax and accept this, knowing that the Lord knows and governs all things. The Lord knows very well what our constitution is, since He caused us to be born of specific parents belonging to a specific family.

Therefore, instead of anxiously focusing on the "why" of our circumstances, we should be much more in prayer about the purpose of our circumstances. I know too well that this is far from being simple, but also that it is more than worth the effort. I know from experience that the Lord is willing to give us what we need, as well as that such circumstances can be beneficial when they are blessed by the God who is mindful of both man and beast and never causes one to seek His help in vain.

Other Devices of Satan

In addition to his activities to make people believe that they have sinned against the Holy Ghost, and thereby to lead them to desperation and desperate acts, Satan frequently manifests his activity in other areas.

I have already mentioned that one of the symptoms of psychological instability is that people are pre-occupied with certain things—particularly things that make them fearful. They do not really want to dwell on these things, but it is as of they are compelled to do so. Whatever they try, they cannot break these thought patterns. This frequently causes them to berate themselves by saying, "You do not want to stop thinking about these things. You want to dwell on these things and therefore your thoughts are ever and again going in that direction." Not only do such people often berate themselves in this fashion, but others will do likewise. It should come as no surprise that this will cause them to feel very inferior and guilty.

Is it really true that such persons want to dwell on that which makes them so anxious? Or could it be that as a result of their psychological condition they no longer have control over their will—that is, that the functioning of their will has been affected by mental instability?

I believe that the latter is the true cause of such compulsory thought patterns. It is therefore entirely misplaced to feel guilty and inferior about this. It is merely a symptom of weakness—just as we have other symptoms due to physical illnesses. By not taking this into consideration, we can torment ourselves and others needlessly.

In his *The Pilgrim's Progress*, Bunyan describes for us what Christian experienced during his journey through the "Valley of the Shadow of Death." As Christian traveled through this valley, he was pursued by demons that whispered all manner of blasphemy in his ears. Christian was deeply troubled by this, for he believed that these dreadful words proceeded from his own heart! Satan and his cohorts took advantage of the circumstances in which Christian found himself to deploy their vicious activities intended to incite despair.

Since "there is one event to the righteous, and to the wicked" (Eccl. 9:2), both God's children as well as the ungodly can be subjected to the insinuations of Satan. The insinuation of blasphemous thoughts and words is also one of the dreadful specialties of the murderer from the beginning by which he has incited anxiety in a countless number of individuals.

I once found myself in such a dreadful situation. I had not yet read Bunyan's *Pilgrim's Progress*. The curse of praying for my own damnation continually went through my mind, and I feared that it would not take very long before that curse and other blasphemous words would come across my lips. My anxiety was increased by words that continually came to mind, "The LORD will not hold him guiltless that taketh his name in vain" (Exod. 20:7). I feared therefore that at any moment I would sink away into perdition. At a given moment it came to mind that the Lord is all-knowing. I said, "Lord, Thou knowest all things. I acknowledge that because of my sins I am worthy of being damned forever, but, Lord, Thou knowest that I do not want to curse and that I am helpless against this compulsion to curse. Thou knowest that my only desire is to be reconciled with Thee and to praise and glorify Thy Name." As a result of calling upon the Lord to be my witness, the snare was broken. Later I read to my amazement in Bunyan's book, and in other writings of the godly, similar experiences in this vale of tears.

Should you be plagued with this compulsion to curse, then you ought to keep this in mind. For indeed, the Son of man has been manifested to destroy the works of the devil. May He use what I have just written so that those who are oppressed and in bondage may receive "beauty for ashes, the oil of joy for mourning, the garment of praise for the spirit of heaviness" (Isa. 63:1)—yes, holy liberty instead of fearful bondage.

Suicidal Attempts

There is yet another category of people who are greatly troubled because of Satan's devices: Those who have made an attempt to commit suicide. Some have attached great significance to the fact that Elijah laid himself down to sleep under a juniper tree, maintaining that a toxic odor emanated from the juniper tree which could even prove to be fatal. The intent is obvious: they wish to suggest that it was Elijah's intent to commit suicide.

I think that this is not the case. First, Elijah prayed to the Lord that his life be taken from him. Furthermore in my research I did not find a single reference to the fact that a juniper tree exudes a toxic odor.[1] I therefore disagree with those who maintain that Elijah made an attempt to commit suicide, and with those that believe only unbelievers attempt suicide. I know of several individuals (of whom some have already died in the Lord) who attempted suicide. The fact that they did not die is only to be attributed to the Lord's gracious intervention, who for His covenant's sake had compassion on them. The fact that the Lord does show compassion toward such needy souls is proof that it is simply not true what some maintain, namely, that an attempt to commit suicide is an unpardonable sin. If the Lord Jesus had also not paid for that sin with His precious blood, salvation would not have been possible for those who have attempted suicide. Their salvation proves that with the Lord there is forgiveness for that sin. The blood of Jesus Christ, God's Son, cleanses from that sin.

It is a known fact that depressive individuals often contemplate suicide. We must not equate the thought to commit suicide with the contemplation of how to commit suicide. Thinking of suicide can be an insinuation of Satan. Countless individuals are plagued with such insinuations. They do not want to yield to such thoughts and would like to get rid of them—but to no avail. Satan, the murderer from the beginning, will leave no stone unturned to assault us and to make us as wretched as possible. We are not accountable for such assaults. We are accountable for yielding to such thoughts and for making suicidal plans.

Many situations can occur in a man's life where he would prefer death above life. God's law, however, forbids the commission of suicide. It is indicative of the depth of our fall that man wants to engage in that which belongs only to God's domain. He has determined both the duration and progression of our lives; contemplating suicide reveals the power of sin and Satan, prompting man to choose a way that is contrary to God's Word and His express prohibition, "Thou shalt not kill." Contemplating suicide also reveals the power of unbelief. The urge to commit suicide does not proceed from God; it flies in the face of God's purposes and will. Therefore to make plans to commit suicide renders one guilty before God. It is, however, not true that there is no forgiveness for that sin. The Lord, being gracious for Jesus' sake, is ready to forgive this sin. By the power of Christ's blood and Spirit we can be delivered.

Not everyone, however, who has attempted and/or succeeded in committing suicide is or was mentally ill. People often make such an attempt to give expression to their despair in the midst of a crisis. Some have done so for attention. When someone feels trapped, feels threatened from all sides, forsaken of God and man, or misunderstood, deceived, and even forsaken—such a person can feel like attempting suicide.

Thinking their situation is beyond change, that forgiveness and salvation are no longer possible, that they have come to a dead end; or that they will have to spend the rest of their lives in dull despair have led many to avail themselves of means to end their lives.

At times those who contemplate suicide will speak about it and at times they will not. The idea that people who talk about their suicidal intentions will not carry out their plans is an error. Reality has proved otherwise. A Swiss researcher maintains that 78% of those who have committed suicide have in one way or another communicated that they were planning to do so. Experts claim that for depressed individuals, the inclination, the urge—or to put it more correctly, the temptation—to commit suicide is greatest at the beginning or near the end of the depression. I have every reason to believe that this is indeed the case. When it becomes apparent that depressed individuals show signs that they will make an attempt to commit suicide, measures will need to be taken to protect them against themselves. This means first of all that the family doctor must be contacted. However, it cannot always be prevented that such persons will nevertheless commit suicide.

When people fail in their attempt to commit suicide, they will have to be counseled in a very tactful manner. The shame of having made such an attempt and the fear of having sinned against the Holy Ghost will press down their shoulders even more than was already the case. How essential it then is to point to the blood of Jesus Christ that cleanses from all sins and to make mention of individuals who, after an attempted suicide, have experienced the forgiveness of sins. In the event that shame and anxiety are absent after a failed attempt, one must be doubly vigilant due to the danger that an attempt to commit suicide will be repeated.

To those whose assessment of people who have attempted suicide is both cruel and harsh, I wish to say, "Let him that thinketh he standeth take heed lest he fall!" They who know from experience what it means to be pursued with the thought that all is lost and that it does not matter whether one arrives in hell a bit sooner than later, will surely refrain from looking down upon those who have committed this act of despair.

Continue to Hope in the Lord

Satan, the murderer from the beginning, often leads people to commit suicide. Suicide is the lowest point in the desecration of man as the image-bearer of God on an earth created and sustained by Him. Satan finds delight in this. As we have already emphasized, he will be particularly ac-

tive in stirring up suicidal thoughts in people who have
great difficulty in coping with life.

For people who are contemplating suicide, the words
of Paul to the jailer are most applicable: "Do thyself no
harm" (Acts 16:28). It is contrary to God's will that we
should harm ourselves. More than that, there is no reason
to do so, for with the Lord there is much forgiveness for
Jesus' sake. The Scriptures tell us that the Lord is near to
those who cry out to Him. Instead of harming one's self,
one must cry out to the Lord—and continue to do so. He
is near, even when we do not sense the nearness of God;
even when there is no change in our anxious circumstances; even when it seems to us that the heavens and the
earth are hard as iron and we do not detect the least relief
upon our prayers. He hears those who expect their salvation from Him. He has promised that He will help those
who come to Him for refuge in all their helplessness.

It may take a long time before the Lord gives some ev-
idence that this is the case—before He causes light to
arise in our darkness. He will indeed manifest His mercy
to those who in all humility cry out to Him and who, regardless of how difficult their circumstances may be,
continue to hope for His goodness. If, however, we no
longer dare to hope upon God's goodness because everything testifies that God will not be merciful, and because
we find in our hearts nothing but iniquity, enmity, rebel-
lion, and bitterness—then what? Even then God's Word
gives us reason to hope continually, for God's promises of
mercy are not founded on any worthiness in man, but
rather, upon the mediatorial work of Jesus Christ who suffered, died, and prays for transgressors.

A despairing person may say, "The Lord Jesus suffered, died, and prays only for His people, and I am not
one of them. I can only consider myself as one of the ungodly. I belong to the reprobates." The Bible states,

however, that the hidden things are to be left with God. We are to concern ourselves with the revealed things. God has revealed in His Word (which is confirmed by oath at holy baptism) that with Him there is abundant forgiveness upon our humble supplication. With that truth we are to be exercised, even though we find that our hearts lack everything that ought to be there and have everything that ought not to be there.

I know what it is to be in such darkness (for a long period of time) that we lose all hope and can only come to one conclusion: no one cares for our soul—no one in either heaven or earth. I also know by experience that there is indeed One who cares for hellworthy and perishing sinners, and that is the merciful High Priest, Jesus Christ.

The Blessedness of Looking to our Merciful High Priest

In Hebrews 4:15, we read that the Lord Jesus was tempted in all things. In all our temptations He has been tempted. There is not anything to which people are subjected to which He has not been subjected. He knows what it means to sink in deep mire in which there is no standing—mire from which one does not know how to escape. He came into deep waters where the floods overflowed Him. He was weary of His crying, and His throat was dried. His eyes failed Him (Ps. 69:2-4). Did not His sweat become as great drops of blood in the Garden of Gethsemane when God laid upon Him the iniquity of us all? He knows what it means to be deserted of God. There is no temptation to which He has not been subjected. Since He, on behalf of sinners, is a merciful High Priest in things pertaining to God, and since He has been tempted in all things, it is impossible for Him not to have compassion with our weaknesses. We are, on that basis, summoned to come boldly to God's throne.

By virtue of Christ's blood which speaks better things than the blood of Abel, God's throne is a throne of grace. What this means is that God can and will be gracious to us for Jesus' sake whenever we, with all our sins and misery, turn to Him for mercy, and to "find grace to help in time of need." God will then, for His Name's sake, give us what we desire of Him. This is not contingent upon any worthiness to be found in us. On the contrary, God has promised that "He will regard the prayer of the destitute, and not despise their prayer" (Ps. 102:17). And He will be true to His Word! Would He say it and not do it? Satan and his cohorts will never be able to say to the Lord in the last day: "These people turned, as utterly destitute ones, to Thee for mercy, and Thou hast permitted them to perish." Jehovah's truth shall stand forever! For His Name and covenant's sake "He shall deliver the needy when he crieth; the poor also, and him that hath no helper.... He shall save the souls of the needy" (Ps. 72:12-13). Therefore, under no circumstances should you harm yourself; and do say to others, "Do thyself no harm."

Suicide is the worst thing we can inflict upon ourselves. Yet it can be so appealing to those who cannot break away from the vicious circle of morbid reflection. Such appeal becomes even greater when we toy with the thought that God in His mercy will forgive us for committing suicide because it was impossible to live any longer. It is very dangerous to entertain the thought that God in His great love and mercy will not consider it a great offense when one in a moment of despair commits suicide. I believe that Satan has snared many people in that trap.

Let us be merciful, however, to those who one or more times have attempted to commit suicide. Their troubles are many as it is. Let us not add more to their burden. We are called to bear one another's burdens and thus fulfill the law of Christ!

I believe that the fact that Elijah laid down under a juniper tree only demonstrates that he was a man who had completely come to the end of his rope, and who, being utterly exhausted and disillusioned, desired to be taken away by the Lord.

Some people hide behind their depression to let others do what they ought to do and are not willing to do themselves, and then they crawl into their beds. That is obviously sinful and should be condemned and resisted. That sort of laying down is of an entirely different nature than what Elijah did. Such people need a different kind of therapy than those who are in a condition such as Elijah was.

---

1 Since the Dutch word for juniper tree is *jeneverboom*, the author makes a connection with the word *jenever*, which is the Dutch word for the alcoholic substance gin. The paragraph that follows relates to that fact and has therefore been excluded. It reads as follows: "They who make such claims are probably influenced by the word gin. This connection is of significance for those who during periods of depression do take refuge to the ginbottle. That is the worst thing one can do under such circumstances. In fact, the drinking of alcohol while taking medication can be fatal. It can be so tempting to take refuge to alcohol in order to escape anxiety, but it does not solve a thing. It will only make the situation worse."

—5—
Sleep and Nourishment

Thus far we have considered what may have and what certainly contributed to Elijah's depression, resulting in his yearning for the termination of his life.

The Lord did not grant Elijah his wish. Elijah believed that death would be his best option. There are many who have been of that opinion during times of deep despondency. Many have gone so far as to attempt suicide but failed because the Lord in His grace and love watched over them and had something better in mind for them.

Instead of letting Elijah die in his wretched condition, the Lord delivered him from his depression. By virtue of His love and covenant faithfulness, the Lord granted him new physical and mental energy and gave him instruction that served for his recovery. We ought not to overlook this; from what Elijah said to the Lord at Mt. Horeb—"I have been very jealous for the LORD God of hosts: for the children of Israel have forsaken thy covenant, thrown down thine altars, and slain thy prophets with the sword; and I, even I only, am left; and they seek my life, to take it away" (1 Kings 19:10)—and from God's response, it is evident that Elijah was entertaining notions that needed correction. The fact that Elijah used the same words twice to express what troubled him the most, proves that he was thinking along certain lines. The same events and facts played a decisive role in the conclusions he drew— conclusions which, among other things, contributed to his depression.

Since Elijah was not a mentally disturbed man, I believe that his deliverance was primarily precipitated by the instruction given to him by the Lord. The Lord corrected Elijah's thought patterns, curing him of his wrong thoughts regarding his usefulness, the fruit his labors, as well as the way the Lord accomplishes His good pleasure in the salvation of sinners. That instruction caused the balance to tip in a favorable direction.

It did not happen suddenly; this can certainly occur, but such was not the case with Elijah. Forty days and nights preceded Elijah's cure from his depression.

All that transpired during those forty days, as well as what took place at Mt. Horeb, culminated in Elijah's recovery. In order that Elijah would acknowledge the error in his thinking and benefit from it, first Elijah's body and spirit had to recover. Many are of the opinion that if it would only please the Lord to speak to their soul by means of His Word, their problems would at once be solved. When this does not occur, they conclude that the Lord has left them alone. From this silence they reason that He has not listened to their prayer for deliverance. They overlook the fact that in order for us to be able to understand what God is saying in His Word, our soul must be in such a state that understanding is indeed possible. A receiver can only receive a signal when the antenna is functioning. As long as it is not, it will not be possible to understand the radio message correctly, nor to respond appropriately to it.

Sleep
It should be noted that the Lord did not begin dealing

with Elijah by speaking to him. The first thing Elijah needed was sleep, for he was completely exhausted. Who knows how long he had been deprived of sleep until he fell asleep under the juniper tree!

In Psalm 127:2 we read, "For so he giveth his beloved sleep." Does this mean that inability to sleep means someone does not belong to the beloved of the Lord? Is this proof that someone has sinned greatly? Is it wrong and sinful to take sleep medication prescribed by a physician? Is this taking refuge to medication rather than to God? During my depression in 1972, I used sleep medication prescribed by my physician, but I wrestled much with these questions. My inability to sleep without medication (in light of what is written about sleep in Psalm 127 and other passages of Scripture), made me very despondent. This was obviously detrimental to the depressed state in which I found myself.

My dependency on sleep medication caused me to believe at that time that I was addicted to this medication, that my faith in God was not of the right sort, and that this was proof of God's displeasure toward me. I now know that this was a device of Satan who also removed this passage from its context, resulting in a wrong perspective. Psalm 127 does not deal with people who are ill, but with healthy individuals who rise up early and sit up late, eat the bread of sorrows, and do not allow themselves rest. In their unbelieving anxiety they will not surrender anything into the hands of the Lord. This therefore refers to an entirely different matter than one's inability to sleep due to physical or mental illness. When all other means fail, the use of sleep medication under the supervision of a physician should not be denounced. With God's blessing this can be beneficial—so much so that afterwards a person will thank the Lord for a season of rest. It is obviously the better option if one can fall asleep without the use of medication; however, when we are compelled to use sleep medication during times when things are out of control for us, it should not be interpreted as something of which we should be ashamed and for which we should be condemned. Those who enjoy good health should refrain from making judgmental statements regarding those who must make use of sleep medication. This will only make them even more despondent. Then we are no longer the Lord's co-laborers, but rather the accomplices of the Prince of Darkness who leaves no stone unturned to lead depressed individuals to despair.

Thus, Elijah needed sleep first and foremost in order to be delivered from his wretched condition.

Many are of the opinion that deliverance from depression is merely a matter of counseling and understanding. Such individuals often want to talk for hours, hoping thereby to be delivered from their problems. Sometimes those who give counsel to the depressed will do everything in their power to persuade them to change their way of thinking by means of lengthy and frequent dialogues, thinking that this will result in healing and restoration. By dialoging with them they do their utmost to extend a helping hand to those who suffer and are often greatly disappointed when such conversations do not yield the desired result. Sometimes they will react to this by rebuking the one who is suffering, thereby causing their suffering to increase.

When depressions are to be attributed to wrong thinking, an erroneous way of judging others, and inappropriate behavior, the depressed person must certainly be counseled. In order, however, for such counseling to be fruitful, the one who suffers must be in a condition to be able to react in a healthy manner to what is said.

There are certain stages of depression in which counseling is of no avail. The only thing one can then do with such a patient is to surround him with love and care until he will be able to react positively to what is being said to him. One of the means would certainly be by prayer for and with him.

When something is wrong with the battery of a car, the problem will be evident. A number of instruments in the vehicle will no longer function as they did before. If we continue to make the same demands on the battery, the battery will become even more depleted. Consequently, the functioning of those parts that are dependent on electricity will become poorer, until finally the battery ceases to function. When certain symptoms indicate that some parts of the vehicle are no longer functioning normally, we seek the help of a qualified mechanic to determine the cause of this—the sooner the better. Once the battery is exhausted, the only solution is to recharge the battery and find the cause of the problem.

There are indications that a person is suffering from physical and/or mental exhaustion. If this is not addressed in a timely fashion and someone insists on demanding from himself or others a performance that can only be expected when he is in good physical and mental health, his condition will obviously deteriorate. If, however, there is a timely response to those symptoms which deviate from the norm, much misery can be prevented through counseling and other measures. Should this be neglected, far greater troubles can be anticipated. A stage may then be reached when counseling will be of no avail. Then the "battery" we need to function normally will need to be recharged. It is my opinion that such was also the case with Elijah. The sleep that Elijah needed was given to him under the juniper tree.

Nourishment

Nourishment was the second thing Elijah needed. How

long must it have been since Elijah ate? The Lord therefore also provided nourishment. How the tender love of the Lord is manifested in 1 Kings 19:5-6! By a miraculous manifestation of His omnipotence, the Lord provided a cake baked on coals and a bottle of water. Yes, more—the Lord sent an angel to touch Elijah to stir him up to arise and to eat. What comfort is couched in the words of David recorded in Psalm 103:13-14, "Like as a father pitieth his children, so the Lord pitieth them that fear him. For he knoweth our frame; he remembereth that we are dust!" This is so beautifully expressed in the rhymed version of this psalm:

> The tender love a father has
> For all His children dear,
> Such love the Lord bestows on them
> Who worship Him in fear.
>
> The Lord remembers we are dust,
> And all our frailty knows.
> —Psalter 278

This is also confirmed by the fact that the angel does not ask Elijah what he asks at a later occasion: "What doest thou here, Elijah?" (1 Kings 19:9). This was not the right moment for that question. What wisdom! How readily and justly the Lord could have heaped rebukes on Elijah instead of providing him with nourishment! Instead, in His great love and mercy, He acted as one would expect a father to act. A judge judges and treats a person according to what he deserves; a father, however, judges and acts in accordance with what a troubled child needs, and only later will discuss the issues that need to be addressed. Without having asked for it, Elijah received what he needed.

Though it is true that many depressed persons do not dare to consider themselves to be children of God and God-fearing people, God's eye looks down in love upon those who desire to fear Him, who cannot achieve what they desire in regard to the fear of the Lord.

—6—
"Arise and Eat"

The Need to Arise

Let us not fail to notice that God's fatherly care also manifested itself in Elijah being told to arise. Elijah was able to arise, and therefore he had to arise. Food was not put into his mouth. Things were not made too easy for him.

It is well-known that depressed individuals usually have no desire to get up to eat or to do anything else. Yielding to this is the way of least resistance, but it is not subservient to the restoration of those who are suffering from deep despondency. A quiet but firm insistence that they do what they are capable of doing is profitable therapy for those who suffer from depression.

Happily, we do not read that Elijah resisted in any way. He could have, for Elijah was a man of like passions as we are. Even converted people can be very recalcitrant when they are called upon to do things they have no desire to do. To be busy with something facilitates physical and mental health. It yields new physical and mental energy, even though they may not be engaged with heart and soul. There are circumstances when people absolutely cannot swallow, even though they very much desire to eat. It would then be entirely out of place to utter rebukes or accusations, implying that such a person is not willing to be healed. It is better to pray for and with such a person. The

Lord has often proven that He is willing to deliver in the hour of need.

What must have gone through Elijah's mind when he ate and drank what the Lord had provided for him in such a special way? This food and drink were certainly visible tokens of the Lord's grace and covenant faithfulness. Whether the seeing and eating of this food and drink had such an effect on Elijah as is so often true for God's children (for example, when partaking of the Lord's Supper), I do not know. Depressed people frequently do not see the value of God's dealings with them, as a result of the malfunctioning of their mental faculties. Once the mind recovers from this mental slump, the ability to assess things in their normal proportions returns. The deeper this slump is, and the longer it lasts, the longer it usually will take before there is full restoration. Recovery will usually occur slowly and intermittently.

Judging by what is written in 1 Kings 19:5, we may assume that Elijah ate and drank silently of the sustenance provided for him. This was consistent with the situation and condition in which Elijah found himself. Was he speechless because he was so amazed? That is possible. Did he not dare to say anything? That is also possible.

Sometimes depressed individuals do not dare to say anything for fear that whatever they say will testify against them. What oppressive anxiety there can be when one neither can nor dares to say anything!

Is it possible that Elijah even neglected to thank the Lord for that which he had received? In any event, it has not been recorded in 1 Kings 19:5. The fact that there is no indication that Elijah gave thanks has been explained in this fashion: that Elijah's heart was too troubled to be able to give thanks. Would that be possible? Can someone's condition be that low (even of a God-fearing man like Elijah) that he will no longer be able to either see or acknowledge any of the Lord's mercies? That is indeed possible.

When we are rebellious about God's leadings in our lives or others', it can occur that we cease to give thanks. When the fire of bitterness rages within, it will consume everything. God's children are then indistinguishable from people of whom the Lord says: "The ox knoweth his owner, and the ass his master's crib: but Israel doth not know, my people doth not consider" (Isa. 1:3). The Lord will not be acknowledged for His benefits.

The depravity of our nature will manifest itself especially when we find ourselves in circumstances contrary to flesh and blood—so much so that at times we will be aghast at ourselves and others. If, by reason of physical or mental weakness, we also lack self-control, things will happen which we had deemed impossible. It will be affirmed time and again that we are incapable of any good and inclined toward all evil. Recalcitrance may coexist with grace; we may even temporarily cease to give thanks for our food and drink. If such is the case, we will indeed have regressed seriously! However, even then we are not to despair of God's mercy. Both history and practice confirm that the Lord will be merciful to sinners for Christ's sake. The Lord Jesus has both suffered and prayed for transgressors—and continues to intercede for sinners. Therefore no one should despair of the possibility of forgiveness and restoration, regardless of how sinful and guilty we are.

The fact that after the consumption of food and drink Elijah laid down once more (probably to continue his sleep) indicates the extent of Elijah's exhaustion. He possibly still did not consider it beneficial to go on living and working and therefore he laid down once more. Depressed individuals frequently succumb to fretting and self-pity. This is wrong, and Elijah may also have been guilty of this.

Another Visit

First Kings 19:7 confirms that the Angel of the Lord removed himself after Elijah's initial consumption of food and drink. A second visit by the Angel of the Lord was necessary to arouse Elijah. What condescending goodness of the Lord it was that the Angel of the Lord came to Elijah once more! How great a mercy this was! This ministry of the Angel of the Lord is a manifestation of the glorious ministry of Christ. From the fact that reference is made twice to the Angel of the Lord, some have concluded that here we have one of the pre-incarnate appearances mentioned in Scripture of the uncreated Angel of the Covenant, the Lord Jesus Christ. In any event, in Elijah's deliverance from his misery we observe the work of Christ as the One who is the Savior of sinners. He who presently leads us time and again in the paths of righteousness for His Name's sake (Ps. 23:3), was already active in the Old Testament as well. To accomplish this, He has the services of both people and angels at His disposal. He is the First and the Last, who will not forsake the works of His own hands. He will turn His hand to the little ones!

At his second visit, the Angel again prompted Elijah to eat. The eating of good and sufficient nourishment is very important. He who neglects this is asking for difficulties. It is a known fact that a decline in physical resilience is closely connected to certain types of depression. Research supports that when there is a recovery of the body's resilience, there will also be a noticeable decline in such depressions. Those who have much experience in this area will therefore heartily recommend that for the recovery of the body's resilience there should be the daily ingestion of good nourishment, supplemented by certain vitamins.

Upon his second visit, the Angel of the Lord spoke more extensively than the first time. At his first visit, the Angel of the Lord only said, "Arise and eat." At his second visit, the Angel of the Lord added these significant words, "because the journey is too great for thee."

This implied that the Lord did not want Elijah to remain at the location where he had laid himself down once more. The words "because the journey is too great for thee" imply that it was the Lord's will that Elijah would arise and proceed to another location. The journey to this location would be too much for Elijah if he were not to eat and drink once more from what the Lord had so lovingly provided for him. There is not a word of rebuke regarding the fact that he had laid down again under the juniper tree. On the contrary, there was only an exhortation to eat and proceed with his journey. The Lord is indeed merciful and very gracious. The Lord did not want Elijah to mope in a corner. Even though Elijah could not see any benefit in continuing to live and to proceed with his journey, the Lord did.

People who are weary of life and totally disillusioned must perceive once more that their life and employment does have a purpose. Though Elijah may have considered himself to be a worthless and useless individual, the Lord was of a different opinion. It was His will that Elijah would continue. It was His intent to replace his oppression with joy—and He still had work for him to do.

When counseling depressed and despondent individuals, every effort must be made to encourage them to believe that there is a task for them to accomplish—in spite of the fact that they think so negatively about themselves and their future. God is both able and willing to use every person for some purpose. Every human being, no matter how weak and discouraged he may be, can, by the Lord's strength and grace, be rendered useful to the benefit of himself and others.

Sometimes it takes a great deal of time and patience to persuade depressed individuals that such is indeed the case. We cannot give them this faith; however, the Lord can bless the words we speak. Then we will observe that they will put their hand to the plough once more, even though they had put aside this "plough" with the intent never to pick it up again, being of the opinion that it would be of no use anyway. What a wondrous book the Bible is indeed! It contains instruction for all the circumstances of life.

— 7 —
A Desire Fulfilled

After having eaten once more and being instructed, Elijah resumed his journey. What would be his destination? The angel of the Lord did not tell Elijah where he should go. Was the reason for this perhaps that Elijah's condition was such that he could not yet handle another assignment? This certainly is a component of therapy administered to people suffering from depression. They may not be left to fend for themselves; they need a certain measure of guidance. Within the context of what is in their best interest, it is wise, however, to leave them alone as much as possible, and to let them do what interests them and go where they choose. This can assist them in gaining or regaining direction for themselves. This is a matter of utmost significance for their recovery, because the deeper the depression, the more listless one will be. However, when there is some improvement, the desire to do something useful will naturally return.

To Mt. Horeb
The fact that Elijah went to Mt. Horeb is an indication that he had the inner desire to go to the place where the Lord had repeatedly revealed Himself. Was this not where the Lord appeared to Moses in the burning bush? It was also the place where the Lord entered into a covenant with

the descendants of Abraham, Isaac, and Jacob—a covenant that the children of Israel had broken. The latter caused so much heartache for Elijah. Mt. Horeb was also the place where the cave was located, of which the Lord said to Moses that there was a place by Him where Moses could have communion with the Lord. It was there that the Lord revealed Himself to Moses as a merciful and gracious God.

A desire to be safe in regard to those who were pursuing him, as well as a desire to have communion with the Lord his God at Mt. Horeb in pouring out His heart to Him and by receiving from His mouth both instruction and comfort—both of these must have motivated Elijah to go to Mt. Horeb.

It is probable that Elijah already planned to go to Mt. Horeb before he lay down under the juniper tree, uttering the prayer that he might die. The words spoken by the angel, "because the journey is too great for thee," appear to dovetail with this. The One who knows the heart and searches the reigns knows what lives in our hearts.

When his depression was at its lowest point, Elijah probably felt that it would be of no benefit to go to Mt. Horeb. He no longer had any desire to go there. It is a horrible thing to be in that state of mind when you have lost interest in everything. Everything appears to be so useless and without purpose. People who have never experienced this have no idea how serious such a situation is. As with so many other things in life, someone must experience it in order to be able to truly identify with what a person can experience in certain circumstances. It is so helpful when people do show a measure of understanding toward people who are depressed; too often, people do not even want to make an effort to gain some insight into what depressed people are going through. Such behavior is deemed to be nothing but the putting on of a show and childish conduct—and often such people make no effort to hide their thoughts. Such conduct is loveless and ungodly. What a stark contrast there is between such a disposition and the loving manner in which the Lord dealt with Elijah and spoke to him! It is the Lord's will that we should bear one another's burdens and thus fulfill the law of Christ (Gal. 6:2).

Even though the Lord did not command Elijah to go to Mt. Horeb, He did not prevent him from going there. It was a good thing that Elijah desired to be at the place where the Lord had previously revealed Himself.

Regardless of how often we have gone astray in life, it is always a good thing to go to the house of the Lord. Satan has everything to gain by keeping us out of the house of the Lord. When we yield to such inclinations, we are aiding and abetting Satan. Even though our being in God's house may be anything but pleasant due to having to hear all manner of things that condemn us, the Lord will yet cause us to hear the voice of His salvation. It pleases Him to instruct those who are going astray and to lead them into the paths of righteousness in His house.

The fact that it took Elijah such a long time to arrive at Mt. Horeb is a matter that calls for reflection. It has been calculated that Elijah could easily have covered the distance to Mt. Horeb in half the time. Should this be attributed to his age, or was this related to the depression that caused him to lie down under the juniper tree? The latter seems the most probable to me. We neither can nor may expect that people who are suffering physically or mentally will, after some refreshment, be able to function as if nothing happened. To demand this of others or ourselves is foolish and unreasonable. And yet, this does happen. We must give others and ourselves the time to recover. Failure to do so will inhibit the healing process. I know that some people would love to run at full speed again—sometimes in order to overcome the feelings of inferiority acquired during the depression. However, in such circumstances, one may not demand of himself or others what can only be performed by people who are in good physical and mental health.

Under normal circumstances Elijah could have made the journey to Mt. Horeb in twenty days or less; now he needed forty days and nights to arrive there. When I was so depressed myself, I said more than once to my wife, "It seems as if all my faculties—my thoughts, will, and ability to act—are paralyzed." It took a long time before this gradually disappeared. As this handicap faded away, I was able to function normally again.

At Mt. Horeb

At last, Elijah arrived where he wanted to be. The Lord provided for Elijah in an extraordinary manner: he had no desire for new food, but nevertheless he had the strength he needed to reach Mt. Horeb.

The wonder of this must not have escaped Elijah. Even though the Lord did not speak audibly to Elijah, He did speak by way of His deeds. By God's dealings with him, Elijah could deduce that the Lord had not left him to fend for himself. How important and profitable it is to take notice of God's voice of providence! This has a therapeutic effect on someone who is inclined to yield to the thought that the Lord has forsaken him.

How great are the mercy and love emanating from the Lord's dealings with Elijah! "Good and upright is the Lord: therefore will he teach sinners in the way" (Ps. 25:8). Elijah and many others have experienced this. It was not for the sake of Elijah's name, but rather for His Name's sake, that the Lord had mercy on Elijah. That Name is the ground in which sinners may cast the anchor of their hope. In all their sins and miseries, they may turn to Him for healing. Do not say to yourself, "I do not dare to do this, for I am not Elijah." In doing so, you will make the gospel of free grace of none effect—to your own detriment. The Lord shows mercy to sinners for Christ's sake alone—for the sake of His covenant that cannot fail. Like David, you ought to say, "For thy name's sake, O LORD, pardon mine iniquity; for it is great" (Ps. 25:11). God has promised that He will hear such prayers for His Name's sake.

It can be deduced from 1 Kings 19:9 that the Lord appeared to Elijah during the first night of his stay at Mt. Horeb. The Lord quickly gave Elijah the desire of his heart. This is not always so, for David sang, "I waited patiently for the Lord" (Ps. 40:1). But the Lord quickly dealt with Elijah as a father deals with a child. He takes him aside when he knows and sees that he is wrestling with problems, asking, "What is the matter with you? Tell me why you are sitting all by yourself in your room." In like fashion, the Lord asked Elijah, "What doest thou here, Elijah?" (1 Kings 19:9). From Elijah's response to that question, it is quite evident that he was still struggling. Clearly, not too much had changed during the forty days and nights that had transpired. The root of Elijah's depression—namely, the error in his thinking and his erroneous manner of assessing everything—was still deeply embedded in his heart. When such is the case, complete restoration by way of sleep, nourishment, and proper care will not happen. There will be a real need for extensive one-on-one counseling to bring about a correction in such a person's thinking and his ability to assess things. To transform Elijah into a man who would again go on his way rejoicing and who would take pleasure in his work, knowing that his labor would not be in vain in the Lord, he had to learn to see things from God's perspective. He had to be cured of thinking erroneously about himself, the fruit upon his labors, and specifically about the manner in which the Lord dealt with him.

Some (such as Matthew Henry) detect in this question ("What doest thou here, Elijah?") a sharp rebuke. I cannot imagine that to be the case. Did not Elijah flee from the land of Israel as a physically and mentally exhausted man due to threatening from powerful Jezebel? God is righteous, indeed, but not harsh. Would not God take into consideration the circumstances that precipitate someone's actions? Not to do so would be merciless. We may not attribute to God a righteousness that is void of mercy. I certainly believe that by way of His question the Lord was calling Elijah to account. He did so, however, within the context of a fatherly interrogation. There is a Dutch proverb that says that the tone makes the music. When we deal with depressed people, let us beware of asking them difficult questions in a harsh tone of voice. This will cause such people to clam up—the opposite of what is needed at such a moment.

At the Lord's question of why he is presently at Mt. Horeb instead of the neighborhood of Mt. Carmel to which the Lord had recently sent him, Elijah pours out his entire heart. How refreshing and therapeutic that can be! How a person can long for the chance to do this! The inability to do so will only increase his anxiety significantly. The pouring out of our hearts is not of our own making, but we can and may ask for it. The Lord has promised to show mercy to those who call on Him, and at His time He will grant this to all who, amid troubles, continue to turn to Him in supplication.

Elijah's Answer

Elijah's response to the Lord's question, "What doest thou here, Elijah?," clearly reveals what was pent up in his heart. The very first thing that becomes evident from his answer is his deep disappointment with his people's sinful behavior toward their faithful covenant-Jehovah.

The other component of Elijah's complaint is his opinion of all the effort he and others had expended on the reformation of a people inclined toward departing from the Lord and His ways. It was Elijah's opinion that he was the only prophet of the Lord left in the land. He knew that there were those who sought to kill him, and when he would die, there would not be a single prophet left. What then would become of the Lord's cause? Was he not therefore justified in having fled? Did not circumstances, as he perceived them, justify his flight and deep despondency? Did they not indicate that the church of the Lord was a dying institution?

Furthermore, Elijah's response to the Lord's question also reveals a deep disappointment about the lack of fruit upon his labors. It is possible that by virtue of his depression Elijah sought the cause partially within himself—although he could truthfully say that he had been very jealous for the Lord's cause. Depressed individuals are inclined to attribute things to their failure, though in reality they are not to be blamed for them. When a congregation refuses to change; when family members or acquaintances refuse to repent; when a family refuses to be subjected to all efforts toward reformation; when all the work a person has done apparently yields no fruit—who would not be dejected, particularly when one has a heart for the Lord's cause? How can it be different when genuine love for the Lord and our neighbor fills our hearts? How bitter the disappointment when, after having made such an all-out effort, we can only conclude that instead of reformation there is increased deformation! Feeling like we have lost the battle after all will be the obvious conclusion. An aggressive zeal toward the misbehavior of others and depression are matters that are often very close to each other.

Some have concluded from Elijah's expression, "I, even I only, am left," a sinful sense of being indispensable. This may indeed have been the case—albeit that depressed people frequently suffer from feelings of inferiority. In any case, one thing is evident from Elijah's answer: He considered his actions as fully justified. From the Lord's response, it was evident that he was mistaken. Elijah was of the opinion that things were truly as he perceived them to be. He was in error. It was true indeed that things had turned out differently than Elijah had thought, wished, and aimed for. The Lord, however, would show Elijah that his assessment of the situation did not agree with reality.

— 8 —
A Divine Answer

The Lord responded to what Elijah said to Him. From the Lord's answer to Elijah it appears to me that the Lord even responded to questions that were in his heart but were not voiced. They were questions such as: "Why did the Lord permit everything to take place as it did?" "Why didn't the Lord prevent the killing of His servants?" "Why didn't the preaching and God's judgments yield fruits worthy of repentance?" Would not all of this have been possible? Was it not reasonable to expect this?

It is so very human (and Elijah was a man of like passions as we are) to wrestle with such questions during times when everything goes so differently than we expected. The concerns about which we dare to speak with God and man can cause our shoulders to droop greatly. However, the questions that we dare not speak to friends, office-bearers, or even the Lord (for the simple reason that, as an insignificant and sinful human being, I dare not ask the Lord for an answer to my question), will weigh us down even more. And yet, such questions need to be answered to lift up the downcast heart and to lift our depression.

How inexpressibly great is the Lord's goodness that in His condescending love He even responds to the questions we do not utter but cause us to weep and sigh! Elijah received an answer rather quickly. That is not always the case, for David speaks in one of his psalms about "spending my years with sighing" (Ps. 31:11).

Before the Lord instructed Elijah audibly, He spoke to him by way of signs—signs such as a great and mighty wind, rending the mountains and breaking the rocks, an earthquake, and a fire reminiscent of God's descent upon Mount Horeb at the giving of the law (Exod. 19:16-18). At Mount Horeb, there were also awe-inspiring displays in the realm of nature designed to inspire humility. That which transpired at that time was here repeated. The God who gave His law and who entered into covenant with Israel was the same God who revealed Himself to Elijah. The God whom Elijah so much desired to meet at Mount Horeb was present. The God whose law was trampled on and whose covenant was broken by Israel showed that He knew all that troubled Elijah's heart. How encouraging it can be when we consider that the Lord knows us and our needs!

However significant and amazing these signs were for Elijah, yet the Lord was not in them. They did not deliver Elijah from his sorrow. That would take place after these signs. The Lord instructed Elijah concerning His good pleasure afterward, and told him the ways that would be subservient to its accomplishment. It is neither by might nor by power that God will accomplish His objective. "My counsel shall stand, and I will do all my pleasure" (Isa. 46:10) By way of a still, small voice, the Lord came to Elijah to instruct him in all this and to deliver him from the pit of destruction into which he had sunk.

It appears that Elijah only expected good things to come by way of mighty things. It appears that he only appreciated the dramatic—that which is visible and audible to all. Being a powerful figure himself whose official ministry was reflected by the display of power in the realm of nature preceding the small still voice, Elijah evidently did not take notice of less dramatic signs. Since Israel's national repentance did not come, Elijah was of the opinion that there had been no conversions at all during his labors and that of other prophets. He was mistaken, however. This becomes evident when the Lord informs him that He left to Himself seven thousand who neither served nor worshiped Baal.

It is also possible that Elijah considered only that to be true conversion which measured up to his ideas and standards. This is an evil that is very prevalent—an evil that in spite of all instruction cannot be eradicated. How much misery has resulted from this! Much depression can be attributed to the measuring of ourselves or others by standards that do not agree with the total context of God's Word. All conversions are powerful—not only those that are accompanied by much distress. In all conversions the almighty power of God is working. Conversions that are not as dramatic as others are no less the work of God than those which are accompanied by great turmoil and change. All who have been or shall be saved will have some knowledge of misery, deliverance, and gratitude (in that order!), but we may not measure the genuineness of a conversion by standards derived from our own experience or that of others. The Lord saw fruit where Elijah did not see it. Elijah needed to be corrected in his manner of thinking and judging. To the Lord's honor and his own well-being, Elijah had to change his way of thinking.

God's speaking to Elijah by way of signs was followed by His speaking to him in words. This was needed so that Elijah would understand the signs and be motivated to put his hand to the plow once more.

Elijah's Commission
The first thing the Lord said to Elijah was, "Go, return on

thy way" (1 Kings 19:15). Elijah fled from Jezreel because he feared he would lose his life by the hand of his enemy. For his own benefit, this root of his anxiety had to be removed first. In the words "Go, return on thy way to the wilderness of Damascus" is implied that Elijah did not have to be fearful at all for those who sought after his soul. He would not perish by the sword of the enemy. His life was in the Lord's hands. No one would be able to kill him. God's counsel shall stand, and He will do all His pleasure (Isa. 46:10). It was as if the Lord said to Elijah, "Fear not; I will help you. I am watching over you and you shall not die by the sword of the enemy. Rather, you shall live in order to do what must be accomplished to My honor and the execution of My good pleasure."

Someone once stated that the entire gospel of God can be summarized in these two words: "Fear not!" In opposition to the multitude of cares and concerns that can so oppress the heart, the Lord places His "Fear not." What great love and compassion emanate from these words! How eminently effective they are, by the power of the Holy Spirit, to banish from the heart anything that oppresses and creates fear! The gospel calls us to believe in Him who is the faithful and mighty One whose grace is so immeasurably great.

To believe means to look away from, to look toward, and to anticipate. Elijah must look away from what threatens his life, look toward the Invisible One, and anticipate His help and assistance. The reason why Elijah did not need to fear was not to be found in Elijah himself. On the contrary, the foundation for this was entirely outside himself in God's Word.

In order for our hearts to be set free from fear, it is necessary to be reminded of this truth time and again. The Lord is pleased to use this to give "the oil of joy for mourning and the garment of praise for the spirit of heaviness" (Isa. 61:3). The prison where we have been sighing will then be opened, and God's perfect love, revealed by His Word and Spirit to the troubled heart, will cast out fear. This is the best medicine. This will yield comfort, spirit, and life to the downcast heart. Depressed people need the pure and simple gospel of God's grace and faithfulness more than anything else. The gospel tells us to look away from everything that presses us down. Look to the Mighty One whom God has given to help sinful people. It calls out to us, "Hope in the God [whoever you may be] who has said, 'Look unto me, and be ye saved, all the ends of the earth'" (Isa. 45:22). That is God's revealed will. That must be our starting point: we are welcome. The Lord excludes no one from this message of salvation. Let us therefore not exclude ourselves from it by the reasoning of unbelief. Bring your unbelieving heart to the feet of Him who said, "Come unto me, all ye that labour and are heavy laden, and I will give you rest" (Mat. 11:28). The yearning for His salvation yields rest; that is, if that yearning is focused on nothing else but His promise. Looking for deliverance elsewhere will not yield rest, but rather, unrest, because one then (often unconsciously) shifts the foundation of one's hope from the divine to that which is of man.

John stated in his first epistle, "He that feareth is not made perfect in love" (1 John 4:18). Perfect love had not been perfected in Elijah. However, his experience at Mount Horeb must certainly have contributed to the fact that the flame of the perfect love of God must have burned fiercely in Elijah's heart—perhaps more fiercely than ever before.

It is a painful and distressing experience when we finally acknowledge that we do not love God perfectly. This is particularly true for those from whose heart the Lord (by the shedding abroad of His perfect love) has banished fear more than once, and who afterwards perceive this fear returning within themselves. We would like to be rid of this fear, but we do not succeed. We feel that by yielding to fear we dishonor and grieve the Lord. This will press us down and make or keep us in a state of despondency. It can be so depressing when we discern within ourselves time and again that we are more ready to believe what Satan, the voices within, and people say, than what the Lord says.

How we all continually stand in need of having the Lord minister grace to us out of the fullness of Christ! This will cause faith to be in exercise and fear will then disappear. Then we will not only believe what the Lord says with our minds, but also with the heart. Elijah certainly knew that the Lord reigns; but, although his soul knew this, his feet were almost gone; his steps had slipped (Ps. 73:2). To prevent this, the Lord spoke to Elijah as He did. Let us pray fervently to Him, so that from our hearts all unmotivated, unholy, and unnecessary fear may be banished and we be made perfect in love!

Elijah was not permitted to remain at Mount Horeb. He had to return to the environment he had fled. He was called to labor there, and he had to devote himself to this task again, depending upon the protection and help of the Lord. He had to put his hand to the plough again. There was yet so much work to be done!

What Elijah Needed to Know

The Lord instructed Elijah that executing His counsel (both negatively and positively) would make use of foreign kings in addition to prophets. God would not let the forsaking of His covenant, the demolishing of His altars, and the killing of His prophets go unpunished. However, He would do so at His own time, not Elijah's time, and in His own manner, not the manner which Elijah deemed the correct way. Things would not go as Elijah wanted them to go, but as God wanted them to go.

What a necessary lesson it is for us to learn to desire less and less that everything would happen according to our wishes! Many depressions are caused by the fact that someone neither can nor will accept that things are turning out so differently than they desire—or believe that they ought to be. Our prayer too often boils down to "my will be done." That needs to be corrected. The Lord Jesus prayed, "Not my will, but thine, be done" (Luke 22:42). That is our example. Let us pray much that we would be conformable to Him in that respect.

Elijah also needed to know that the Lord would not visit Israel only with the rod and bitter affliction. Both Hazael of Syria and Jehu of Israel would indeed wield the sword so that God's impugned authority would be vindicated; even Elisha would be used to vindicate God's justice and to execute judgment. Elisha's work, however, would consist primarily in prophesying. In light of what God communicated at Mount Horeb, Elisha's work would be characterized primarily by the sign of the still, small voice. The Lord would come in this to lead sinners in the pathway of righteousness. Elisha would reap what Elijah had sown.

There was still a future for Israel's church. Elijah needed to know this. This is often a remedy for depression. If we only focus on the here and now, who would not become despondent? When we consider the proliferation of wickedness today, we will inevitably begin to think and say, "The world and the church are perishing." However, is it not written that Jehovah's truth shall stand forever, and that His covenant bonds will not sever? God will uphold His work and His church. It is a different matter that this goes differently than we imagine. As human beings we are so inclined to think according to certain set patterns; if something does not fit that pattern, we become despondent. We need to be cured of this. May the remedy the Lord administered to Elijah by instructing him also have a blessed effect on us.

There is no doubt that, in speaking to Elijah, the Lord gave an explanation of what preceded that speaking. The fact that the Lord was not in the strong and mighty wind that rent the mountains and broke the rocks, and the fact that He was also not in the earthquake and the fire, were explained by the Lord as He addressed Elijah. Neither the strong wind, nor the earthquake, nor the fire yielded that which Elijah yearned for so much. The strong wind, the earthquake, and the fire did, however, have their effect.

Was Elijah's zeal for the Lord depicted in the awe-inspiring natural phenomena? Was not Elijah's despondency caused by the absence of the so sorely desired national repentance of the children of Israel? In any event, the Lord instructed Elijah that the labors of Elijah and the prophets had not been entirely without effect. Even though their labors had not precipitated a national repentance, the Lord had yet used those labors so that seven thousand people remained who did not bend the knee to Baal nor render idolatrous worship to him. Elijah's labors had been more fruitful than he thought. In his despondency, Elijah thought that nothing good had been accomplished by all the work he had done. How mistaken he was! It had, with God's blessing, accomplished more than he anticipated.

It is often hidden from the sowers of God's Word how much fruit there has been upon their sowing in the home, in the extended family, among friends, at work, or in the congregation. Knowing it could make us proud; everyday experience confirms this. A feather still needs some wind to elevate itself from the ground, but our proud natures elevate themselves effortlessly. Our proud ego must be brought down and be kept there, so that no one would glory except in the Lord. However, when our heart is despondent because no fruit is seen, the Lord will frequently let us know that our labor with God's Word has not been in vain. What a blessed effect this has on a despondent heart! Elijah needed this to be delivered from his depression, and to regain the joy and courage needed to live. In what a fatherly fashion did the Lord encourage a grieving Elijah who was so weary and burned out!

When someone is not discouraged, we do not need to let him know of how much benefit he or she is for the family, the church, and society at large. When people are despondent, however, because they consider themselves so useless and fruitless, it is necessary to point out the good that has been accomplished through them. That can be a blessing that the Lord is pleased to use to lift up weary hearts.

There are people who are of the opinion that it is wisest to never speak positively about someone's accomplishments. They never utter an encouraging word to their husband or wife, their children, or anyone else; they only point out the things that are lacking. This, however, is not wisdom, but foolishness. The Lord only knows how many people have been victims of such foolishness. Let my soul not follow such individuals. They will one day have to give an account of their wretched conduct to Him who judges without respect of persons. If converted people make themselves guilty of such conduct, spiritual leanness and darkness will be their portion in this life. Woe to them who discourage those who need encouragement! Those who are guilty of pushing despondent people deeper into the pit of despair will end up in this pit themselves. God is not an idle observer of what we do, nor does what we say escape Him. There are people who are of the opinion that it does not matter if you step on a blade of grass; they say that what is alive will always recover. It has probably never occurred to them that there are "blades of grass" who are permanently damaged and who will never recover. Thus there are people (even among God's children) whose lives have been harmed by the misbehavior of others, and who sometimes suffer the consequences their entire lives. Let us learn from the Lord's way of dealing with Elijah that an encouraging word in due season is a good matter. Paul, moved by the Holy Spirit, also did so several times in his letters.

As He instructed Elijah, the Lord also addressed the fact that Elijah had said that he alone had remained of all the prophets. Would Elijah, by virtue of his depression, have lost sight of the hundred prophets who, according to the word of Obadiah (1 Kings 18:4), had hid themselves in a cave and were sustained with bread and water by Obadiah? That is very well possible. When we are preoccupied with ourselves and our circumstances, we will lose sight of all the good that still may be there due to the grace of God. Depressed people only focus on what, in their opinion, is lacking. It is possible for someone to become depressed as a result of negative thought patterns. And sometimes being depressed makes us judge everything negatively.

It is possible that Elijah thought that, at his death, the generation of prophets would have died out. If that were so, then it is understandable that he sank away into the miry clay. Who would not sink away in deep despondency when considering that the end of all things is near?

By stating that only he was left of the prophets of the Lord, Elijah could also have meant that he was the only prophet who still openly testified against the sins of the house of Ahab and those of the nation of Israel. Some explain Elijah's statement to mean that Elijah was of the opinion that he was the only believer who was left. That seems to me to be a bit far-fetched—albeit depressed people can at times make the most bizarre statements. It serves no purpose to respond to this with harsh words of rebuke; it is better to counter such negative statements with something positive. Such was the Lord's approach with Elijah. He commissioned Elijah to anoint Elisha as prophet—which did not mean that Elijah was dismissed from the Lord's service. The rest of this history proves that the Lord continues to use Elijah as prophet. What it did confirm is that the Lord made provision that the prophetic office would not cease. The prophetic ministry would continue—also without Elijah.

What Elijah did not know, however, and needed to know to fully recover from his depression, was that there was a God-fearing Elisha whom God had prepared and equipped to succeed Elijah. Indeed, the situation was much more positive than Elijah believed it to be! How beneficial such instruction and good news can be to deliver the despondent heart from paralyzing pessimism! God's covenant with Abraham His friend cannot be annulled. His promises cannot fail, no matter what the circumstances are. God will not alter that which has gone out of His lips (Ps. 89:34), although the heirs of these promises may better deserve the Lord's retraction of His promises. He will indeed take vengeance of their inventions (Ps. 99:8), but Satan, the world, and their own sinful nature will not be the victors in this battle. God's cause will triumph! As long as the sun and moon shall endure, sinners, by way of the ministry of the Word, shall be drawn out of darkness into God's marvelous light. When we see the power, grace, and faithfulness of the Lord, the health of our countenance will be restored.

The Lord showed Elijah both visibly and audibly that he will not allow sin to go unpunished. There would indeed be people who would perish, but death would not have the last word. The Lord does indeed chastise—but not endlessly. Upon the stormy wind and the earthquake follows the still, small voice. God vindicates His honor in the way of justice and grace—but in such a way that His grace will ultimately triumph. The still, small voice will bring about what Elijah has yearned for so fervently. The Lord is pleased to use one person for one task and another for a different task. The one plows, the other sows, and another reaps. The one whom the Lord uses to plow is not less than the one whom He is pleased to use to sow and to reap. Everyone ought to be satisfied with the place and task the Lord has given him. To be dissatisfied with that which the Lord has sovereignly designated for us will only yield grief. "None can stay his hand, or say unto him, What doest thou?" (Dan. 4:35). Failure to accept ourselves and our limitations, and failure to accept the place and task to which the Lord has appointed us, can precipitate depression. It will bring us into bondage. When, however, we accept the place and task of the Lord's appointment, the joy of liberty and happiness will be our portion. The blessing of the Lord yields such liberty and happiness, and it will cause us to delight ourselves in the discharge of the obligations to which we are called by God's precepts and providence.

The Lord Jesus was willing to merit this blessing for sinful creatures who, in and of themselves, are unwilling and unfit to accept this. His blood cleanses from all sins, and by His Spirit He will deliver us from resisting His will and will stir us up to follow Him humbly and joyfully, amazed that the Lord is pleased to use us in any capacity at all. It is the Lord's will that we should ask Him to give us what He demands from us. He has never said, "Seek ye me in vain" (Isa. 45:19). He who continues to call upon the Lord in truth (Psa. 145:18), will experience that He will hear the needy when they cry, for His Name's sake.

This has been the experience of countless men and women. In Elijah's case we do not even read that he prayed, and yet the Lord was merciful to him. He did not do this because Elijah was a special person. On the contrary! He was a man of like passions as we are—a truth the Lord has emphatically recorded in His Word (James 5:17). It was only for Christ's and His covenant's sake that the Lord was mindful of Elijah.

No one can say, "I am not Elijah, and thus there is no message or comfort in what he experienced." By teaching us to see Elijah as a man of like passions as we are, the Lord is speaking to all who either read or hear of the history of Elijah's life. His entire life is a continual testimony of the greatness of God's grace manifested toward a wretched sinner in whom there was no reason why God should have been gracious to him. He did so purely for Christ's sake—for the sake of His eternal good pleasure and because it sovereignly pleased Him that it should be so. What a joyful message and encouragement this contains for people who are of like passions as Elijah, as we all are! Hope in God, for you shall yet praise him for the salvation wrought by the power and blood of Christ.

The conclusion of the Lord's speech to Elijah also confirms that His good pleasure will prosper through Christ. How the heart of Elijah must have been filled with amazement and joy when he heard the Lord's testimony, "Yet I have left me seven thousand in Israel, all the knees which have not bowed unto Baal, and every mouth which hath not kissed him" (1 Kings 19:18). Though it was true that these seven thousand constituted only a small minority compared to the majority of apostates, yet it was a large and full number. God's counsel will stand and He will do all His pleasure (Isa. 46:10). This is the ground into which we may cast the anchor of our hope. This is medicine for depression. This enabled Elijah to go on.

Faith in God's truth and faithfulness will give us courage to continue on the pathway of life. It will also give us the desire to continue with our labors, for such faith yields new strength.

— 9 —

From Complaint to Doxology

From the remainder of 1 Kings 19 and other passages of Scripture, it is evident that the word of the Lord to Elijah at Mount Horeb was instrumental in delivering Elijah fully from his depression. His youth had been renewed as the eagle's (Ps. 103:5). We read in 1 Kings 19:19, "So he departed thence...." The man who six weeks earlier wished to die, once again had courage and strength to run the race set before him. Having been delivered from fear for his enemies, having surrendered to the Lord's dealings with him and others, and having been strengthened by the Word and Spirit of the Lord, Elijah went back to work. The truth of Psalter 317 verse 2 was true for him:

> The Lord with me, I will not fear
> Tho' human might oppose;
> The Lord my helper, I shall be
> Triumphant o'er my foes.

Back to Work
No matter what the task is that the Lord has called us to in our families, churches, and society at large, what a wonderful thing that we can do our work! Both our work and our life have meaning then. When we believe that our

labor has never been and never will be in vain in the Lord, and when we know that the Lord's eye is always upon us, our feet will be like hinds' feet (Ps. 18:33). Faith in God's promises and faithfulness and the experience of God's compassionate love in Christ gave Elijah the strength to carry out what God directed him to do. However unpleasant his experiences of previous weeks may have been, they enriched his life and strengthened his faith. During these weeks, he has learned lessons that benefitted him and others, and he was grateful to the Lord his entire life. All things must work together for good to those who love God, because He first and continually loved them in spite of their sins and failures.

Such love will stir us up to reciprocate; and such reciprocal love causes us to exclaim, "Nevertheless I am continually with thee: thou hast holden me by my right hand" (Ps. 73:23). To think that He held my hand—the hand of one so sinful, so wretched, so doubting, so despondent, so foolish, and so inclined to depart from His ways! That is a wonder of wonders! To think that the Lord neither cast us away nor dismissed us from His service, leaving us over to ourselves, and instead has seen fit to use us in His service—what unmerited favor indeed!

The history of Elijah has been recorded for our learning. His story identifies the dangerous rocks we must avoid to the utmost of our power. If a strong believer such as Elijah came into such a deep pit of misery, it can also happen to us. "Wherefore let him that thinketh he standeth take heed lest he fall" (1 Cor. 10:12).

If, however, you have come into the depths of despondency and fatigue, you ought not to think that this cannot happen to true believers. You also ought not to think that you can no longer be delivered. So many have thought, "I will never get out of this; I am useless," etc. Yet, they have experienced, just like Elijah, that God has turned the shadow of death into the morning (Amos 5:8). They have also experienced that "His arm protects His people who on His power rely (Psalter 183:4, Ps. 68). Before God's throne and here below there is a great multitude which praises God "for the plenitude of His boundless magnitude" (Psalter 430:1, Ps. 150).

These people are of like passion as we are, and they did not experience God's salvation because they made themselves worthy of it. No, it was only because of the Lord's sovereign good pleasure that He was mindful of them and cared for them. Therefore, be encouraged by their deliverance—to God's honor and your salvation. Perhaps you say, "I neither can nor dare to be encouraged by their deliverance, because I am not like they are; I simply am not able to take courage from this." You should know that they did not have this from themselves. Their eyes poured out tears to God (Job 16:20), and the Holy Spirit enabled them to do this. "If ye then, being evil, know how to give good gifts unto your children: how much more shall your heavenly Father give the Holy Spirit to them that ask him?" (Luke 11:13).

Delivered from Bondage

In Psalm 116:9, we read: "I will walk before the Lord in the land of the living." These could also have been the words of Elijah. This is the language of everyone the Lord sets free from bondage. We are not told who the poet of Psalm 116 is. We assume it was David, but it could just as well have been someone else. It is not essential for us to know who wrote this psalm. For people who say, "I am neither like David nor like others who are mentioned by name," it can be so helpful to read a psalm written by an author we do not know. The essential thing is that the Holy Spirit inspired the poet of Psalm 116 to write words that have instructed, comforted, and saved countless men and women.

When the poet wrote this psalm, he had just been through a very difficult time. It was a time when the sorrows of death compassed him and the pains of hell had hold of him. It was a time when he sought to do good, and instead he "found trouble and sorrow" (Ps. 116:3); and in verse 6, he states that he was brought low. Completely exhausted, with death staring him in the face and his tears for his food and drink, he dragged himself from one day into the next (v. 8). He was greatly afflicted during this period (v. 10). What could have caused all this trouble?

All of this could surely have been the result of sin. When we experience that we have greatly offended God and have departed from His ways, when God's hand is heavy on us day and night, and when we feel the fire of God's wrath burn within us, then our moisture will be turned into the drought of summer (Ps. 32:4). My bones wax old through my roaring all day long (Ps. 32:3), and the sorrows of hell will rob me of all comfort.

However, it is also possible that the sins of others bring us into such wretched circumstances. Psalm 116:11 leads me to believe this was why the poet found himself in such a predicament. We read, "I said in my haste, All men are liars." I therefore conclude that the lies of people—the untrustworthiness of people the poet would never have expected to betray him—caused him to be compassed by the sorrows of death and held by the pains of hell. Other believers could possibly have brought him into the circumstances that led him so close to death with eyes red from tears.

What a terrible shock it can be when we find ourselves in distressful circumstances due to the dishonesty of people whom we esteemed so highly, in whom we had unlimited trust because of their reputation or the office they held! Our trouble is not only caused by external circumstances, but what is worst of all, by people from whom we did not expect such conduct. That makes it a double blow and makes us sink in the miry clay. In anger and deep sorrow, we cry out, "Is there anyone who is upright? Faithfulness and truth are not to be found among men."

Someone wrote, "Even if the poet of Psalm 116 would not have spoken in haste, he would have been correct in saying that all men are liars." We may not, however, paint all people with the same brush. To our benefit, the poet himself acknowledged this a bit later.

What trouble has been brought in this world because of lies! James wrote that "the tongue...is an unruly evil, full of deadly poison" (James 3:8). I once witnessed how the little fire of a cigarette butt changed a beautiful field into a black and charred area. I have also witnessed the destruction caused by tongues. I have personally been compassed by the sorrows of death and the pains of hell due to false claims people had made. How desperately we need to pray daily with David, "Set a watch, O Lord, before my mouth; keep the door of my lips" (Ps. 141:3); and with Agur, "Remove far from me vanity and lies" (Prov. 30:8)! Lies not only cause grief to others, but also bring great trouble to us, for "however swift the lie may be, the truth will gain the victory" (Dutch proverb). Even if people will not expose our lies, the Lord will expose them.

Nevertheless, it is a dreadful thing when the lies of others bring people into the depth of misery. What deep wounds can be inflicted by our words! What wounds can be inflicted to the heart when our trust in people, who we never expected to do what they did, has been shattered—wounds that are more painful than physical wounds! Psychiatrists and others who are engaged in alleviating psychological stress are extending a helping hand every day to people who have become severely depressed due to ex-

periences similar to those of the poet of Psalm 116. May it
comfort such people to know that what they are going
through has been experienced by others who were delivered from trouble by the Lord. The Savior had mercy upon
the one who wrote Psalm 116, enabling him to write a doxology in which he, to the benefit of others, magnified the
wondrous deeds of the Lord. When he found himself in
deep trouble, he could not have thought that the day
would come in which he would sing a doxology such as
this. But it happened! The Savior who as Surety had to endure all manner of suffering in order to make payment for
the sins of His people, and who by His power helps those
who suffer due to their own sins or the sins of others—this
Savior still lives to deliver the needy from all their troubles.

In his great need, the poet of Psalm 116 called upon
the name of the Lord. He cried out, "O Lord, I beseech
thee, deliver my soul" (v. 4). His prayer was short. It has
been said that the greater the need, the shorter the prayer.
This does not mean, of course, that longer prayers, particularly those that are poured out in secret before the
countenance of the Lord, are of a lesser quality. Neither
length of prayer nor certain wordings are a prerequisite
for receiving God's help. It is not due to the quality of our
prayer, but it is for His Name's sake that the Lord is merciful to us in response to our prayers. The poet took refuge
to God in his distress, for people had betrayed him. He
could not rely upon their words and their promises. However, the Lord God, whose Name is the warranty of His
words, said, "Call upon me in the day of trouble: I will deliver thee" (Ps. 50:15), and He neither can nor shall lie.
Would He ever not mean what He says? "Hath he said,
and shall he not do it?" (Num. 23:19).

What a blessing that the Lord has so many names!
Every one of these names has suitable applications for a variety of circumstances. His covenant Name Yahweh

(Jehovah) is especially suitable to sustain people who have become disillusioned with everything outside of God. Even when sorrows and pains of our own sins overwhelm us, God's Name will encourage us to turn to Him for deliverance from all our sins and miseries. His Name guarantees that for the sake of His Name and His Son He shall not turn away the prayer of those who cry out from the depths with heart and soul to Him for grace and mercy.

This does not mean, however, that help and deliverance will always be experienced immediately, even though they can be sometimes. In Psalm 34:4-6 we read, "I sought the Lord, and he heard me, and delivered me from all my fears. They looked unto him, and were lightened: and their faces were not ashamed. This poor man cried, and the Lord heard him, and saved him out of all his troubles." However, in Psalter 108:1 (Psalm 40) we read, "I waited for the Lord my God, Yea patiently drew near, and He at length inclined to me, my pleading cry to hear."

Brought up out of the Miry Clay

It seems probable to me that the poet of Psalm 116 was not immediately delivered from his distressful circumstances. A person is not "brought low" (v. 6) overnight. The poet possibly only began to cry out to the Lord when he was brought low. In the crucible of life, both experiences are common. Whatever may have been the case, however, the Lord delivered the poet from the horrible pit and the miry clay. According to verse 10, it was through faith that the soul of the poet was delivered from death and his eyes from tears (v. 8). The Lord evidently enabled the poet, by His Spirit, to take hold of Him and His Word. The Lord granted him grace for grace out of the treasury of the covenant of grace. "Jehovah's kindly face gives happiness and grace" (Psalter 423:7). It transforms the shadow of death into a place of rejoicing. Jacob speaks of this: "I have seen God face to face, and my life is preserved" (Gen. 32:30).

The poet attributed his deliverance to God's grace and righteousness (v. 5). He knew all too well that there was nothing in himself to deserve God's mercy. He was only a poor sinner. However, it was true that he had been falsely accused. Before God, he had no personal righteousness, but his cause was a righteous one. In Psalm 18:20-21, David said, "The Lord rewarded me according to my righteousness; according to the cleanness of my hands hath he recompensed me. For I have kept the ways of the Lord, and have not wickedly departed from my God."

All too often, however, we lay claim to neither our personal righteousness nor the righteousness of our cause when we cry to God out of the depths. Our hearts accuse that we are to blame; that is why the sorrows of death and the pains of hell overwhelm us. This makes our circumstances doubly distressing. How can a righteous God deliver us from destruction? He can because of His grace and righteousness. God is not only righteous in punishing sin, but He is also righteous in fulfilling His promises. In harmony with His righteousness (or justice) and for the sake of the obedience of Christ, He will bless those who turn to Him with their sins and miseries. No—more than that: that is how His righteousness is magnified. When we put our trust in Christ's atoning blood and righteousness by a faith that the Lord works in the heart by His Spirit, take refuge in His work as the Mediator, and hold on to God's faithfulness in fulfilling His promises, then our souls will be set at liberty.

It can take time before a soul, crying to God out of the depths, will experience such liberty. Yet, "your heart shall live, ye saints that seek the Lord; He helps the needy and regards their cries, those in distress the Lord will not despise" (Psalter 187:3).

When we humbly supplicate for mercy for Christ's sake, whose blood speaks better things than that of Abel, our prayers will not go unanswered. In God's time, those who seek His grace will find it, for "gracious is the Lord, and righteous; yea, our God is merciful" (Ps. 116:5).

When it comes to glorying in God's grace and righteousness, all who have been blessed by God will be of the same kindred spirit. They will be of one mind; Psalm 116 articulates exactly what their hearts speak. We do not have a psalm of Elijah in which he sings of his deliverance from bondage. But would he not have agreed wholeheartedly with the poet of Psalm 116? Perhaps in somewhat different words, but he would have said with all the redeemed of the Lord, "I will walk before the Lord in the land of the living.... What shall I render unto the Lord for all his benefits toward me? I will take the cup of salvation, and call upon the name of the Lord. I will pay my vows unto the Lord now in the presence of all his people" (Ps. 116:9, 12-14).

To walk before the Lord, to commemorate His wondrous deeds of old, and to meditate upon His work (Psalter 212:5, Ps. 77) is a God-glorifying and blessed activity. It was the choice of the poet of Psalm 116 to reciprocate God's love by walking before Him and by keeping His law diligently—regardless of any opposition he might meet. This was also the choice of Elijah, and the choice of all who experience, "He hath heard my voice and my supplications....He hath inclined his ear unto me."

This choice is a wholehearted one, though the outworking of it will regrettably be partial at best in this life. The complaint, "O wretched man that I am! who shall deliver me from the body of this death?" (Rom. 7:24), proceeds from the lips of the Lord's people as long as they live. However, the words "I thank God through Jesus Christ our Lord" will also continue to be heard. The Lord

Himself will see to this. By God's grace and power, there will always be people who sing,

I love the Lord, the fount of life and grace;
He hears my voice, my cry and supplication,
Inclines His ear, gives strength and consolation;
In life, in death, my heart will seek His face.

—Psalter 426:1

In writing this book, I have also sought to pay my vows to the Lord who time and again delivered me and who commissioned me to "comfort the feebleminded" (1 Thess. 5:14). "Blessed be the Lord God, the God of Israel, who only doeth wondrous things. And blessed be his glorious name for ever: and let the whole earth be filled with his glory; Amen, and Amen!" (Ps. 72:18-19).

CPSIA information can be obtained
at www.ICGtesting.com
Printed in the USA
FFHW02n1333190918
48495280-52351FF

9 781892 777935